AF255795

THEODORE BEZA

CASCADE COMPANIONS

The Christian theological tradition provides an embarrassment of riches: from Scripture to modern scholarship, we are blessed with a vast and complex theological inheritance. And yet this feast of traditional riches is too frequently inaccessible to the general reader.

The Cascade Companions series addresses the challenge by publishing books that combine academic rigor with broad appeal and readability. They aim to introduce nonspecialist readers to that vital storehouse of authors, documents, themes, histories, arguments, and movements that comprise this heritage with brief yet compelling volumes.

OTHER TITLES IN THE SERIES:

Reading Paul by Michael Gorman
The Rule of Faith by Everett Ferguson
The Second-Century Apologists by Alvyn Pettersen
Origen by Ronald E. Heine
Athanasius of Alexandria by Lois Farag
Basil of Caesarea by Andrew Radde-Gallwitz
Reading Augustine by Jason Byassee
A Guide to St Symeon the New Theologian by Hannah Hunt
Thomas à Kempis by Greg Peters
Lutheran Theology by Paul R. Hinlicky
John Calvin by Donald K. McKim
Martin Bucer by Donald K. McKim and Jim West
Heinrich Bullinger by Donald K. McKim and Jim West
Jacob Arminius by Rustin E. Brian
Richard Hooker by W. Bradford Littlejohn
John Wesley by Henry H. Knight III
A Companion to Mercersburg Theology by William B. Evans
Reading Kierkegaard I by Paul Martens
Reading Bonhoeffer by John W. Matthews
Rudolph Bultmann by David W. Congdon
Jacques Ellul by Jacob E. Van Vleet and Jacob M. Rollinson
Understanding Pannenberg by Anthony C. Thiselton

THEODORE BEZA

An Introduction to His Life and Theology

DONALD K. McKIM
JIM WEST

 CASCADE *Books* • Eugene, Oregon

THEODORE BEZA
An Introduction to His Life and Theology

Cascade Companions

Copyright © 2023 Donald K. McKim and Jim West. All rights reserved. Except for brief quotations in critical publications or reviews, no part of this book may be reproduced in any manner without prior written permission from the publisher. Write: Permissions, Wipf and Stock Publishers, 199 W. 8th Ave., Suite 3, Eugene, OR 97401.

Cascade Books
An Imprint of Wipf and Stock Publishers
199 W. 8th Ave., Suite 3
Eugene, OR 97401

www.wipfandstock.com

PAPERBACK ISBN: 978-1-6667-7164-0
HARDCOVER ISBN: 978-1-6667-7165-7
EBOOK ISBN: 978-1-6667-7166-4

Cataloguing-in-Publication data:

Names: McKim, Donald K. [author]. | West, Jim [author].

Title: Theodore Beza : an introduction to his life and theology / Donald K. McKim and Jim West.

Description: Eugene, OR: Cascade Books, 2023 | Series: Cascade Companions | Includes bibliographical references.

Identifiers: ISBN 978-1-6667-7164-0 (paperback) | ISBN 978-1-6667-7165-7 (hardcover) | ISBN 978-1-6667-7166-4 (ebook)

Subjects: LCSH: Bèze, Théodore de, 1519–1605. | Theology. | Theology, Doctrinal—History—16th century. | Reformation—France.

Classification: BX9419.B4 M35 2023 (paperback) | BX9419.B4(ebook)

11/27/23

In honor of Jon Balserak
In glad appreciation for his splendid scholarship
And in deep gratitude for our friendships
through the years.

We are put in the world to serve the glory of God with both body and soul.

—**Theodore Beza,** *Sermons sur l'historie de la Passion* (Geneva: Jean le Preux, 1592), 480.

Whatsoeuer ye doe, doe all to the glory of God.

—**1 Cor 10:31** Geneva Bible, 1599

CONTENTS

ACKNOWLEDGMENTS

Of the making of books there is no end, opined the jaded and grizzled author of the book known as Ecclesiastes, or according to its Hebrew title, Qoheleth. And everyone who has ever written a book knows how very true that is.

Books never seem to end. Not in terms of their composition and writing and editing and publishing, all of which do come to an end eventually. No, rather in terms of their reading, reception, acceptance, or rejection. New readers pick up new books and read them and the more observant among them will find typos and errors that not only have the authors overlooked even through several goes but editors and other readers as well. Books are in need, accordingly, of what seems to be everlasting adjustment.

No book has ever been written that stood or stands as the "last word" on any subject of human investigation. This book, and the others that Don and Jim have written in a collegial and beneficial partnership, is not the last word on Theodore Beza. Nor should it be. And we certainly hope that it isn't.

Many people need to be acknowledged as principal actors in the conception, birth, publication, and reading of this little contribution to Beza scholarship. First, Jim wishes to thank Don, once again, for his genuine collegiality and fraternity. Jim also wishes to thank, as always, his wife, Doris, and his daughter, Rachel, for being enthusiastic about a project which, it's fair to say, is not even of remote interest to them. They are very indulgent of Jim's various interests.

Don would like to thank Jim for his unfailing competence and good humor as we sought to navigate the intricacies of Beza's theology. Working with Jim on these projects has been a wonderful experience and thanks abound!

Don would also like to thank Ann Wallace, Reference Librarian of the Germantown Community Library for generous help in obtaining research resources. Don also thanks Jessica Holland, Library Director of the L. M. Graves Memorial Library of Harding School of Theology, Memphis, for her kindnesses in granting library access and research help along the way.

Don thanks his wonderful wife, LindaJo, for ongoing love and support in our lives together, every day. Our sons and their families bring us joy. We are grateful for Stephen and Caroline and their children, Maddie, Annie, Jack, and Ford. We thank God for Karl and Lauren and all the blessings of family love. Our gratitude to God is deep and enduring.

Both Jim and Don would also like to extend a word of appreciation to our genius editor at Wipf and Stock, Robin Parry. He is simply the best editor in the business, bar none. Naturally we also wish to thank the publisher for bringing this work to the public. Stephanie Hough was a wonderful copy editor and Savanah N. Landerholm has been splendid with typesetting and other editorial helps. We are most grateful to her. Along with our previous books on Bullinger and Bucer, we feel as though we can now turn to other things, having dealt with the big three B's of Reformed theology.

This book is happily dedicated to our fellow Reformation scholar, Dr. Jon Balserak. Jon is an industrious and highly competent researcher and writer. We have benefited greatly from his scholarship through many years. Even more, we both count him as a treasured friend whose company we have enjoyed. Jon is always helpful and full of life-giving energy to encourage us along our ways. We are grateful for Jon in many ways; and are very pleased to dedicate this book in his honor.

Finally, we want to thank you, our reader. The greatest honor an author can have is to be read. And we thank you for your interest. Without you, there are no books.

If Beza is a little better understood and a little more appreciated in the English speaking world, this little book will have served its purpose well. To the Everlasting Glory of Almighty God.

Jim West, Petros, Tennessee
Donald K. McKim, Germantown, Tennessee
August 2023

INTRODUCTION

Welcome to Theodore Beza! We are happy to present this book as a "gateway to Theodore Beza"!

Beza (1519–1605) may not be very familiar since he is not a well-known figure in church circles. This sixteenth-century Protestant reformer became the successor to the famous John Calvin (1509–1564) as the lead reformer in Geneva, after Calvin's death. He was very active in all areas of the church's theology and life in Geneva. Our introductory chapter on Beza's life will acquaint you with the wide range of activities with which Beza was involved.

Beza was a significant theologian in what became the emerging Reformed theological tradition, sometimes also called "Calvinism." His theological work was presented in a systematic form which reflected contemporary intellectual practices. It drew on both humanist and scholastic methods. Beza explored theological questions and provided detailed understandings of them.

Beza's treatment of theological issues emphasized theological insights that continue to be important for Christians. He developed these not only in relation to his reading of holy Scripture and the church's theological traditions but also in the context of his own ministries in Geneva. Beza served as a pastor and carried out pastoral tasks to meet the needs of Christians persons in the city. As one scholar noted, Beza "understood himself to be a pastor. This aspect of his self-understanding influenced the manner in which he instructed and counseled others. He preached several times a week for most of his life as a Protestant. His pastoral vision emerged in his labors as a shepherd of God's flock."[1] Despite the intricacies of Beza's theological discussions, at points, it is important to recognize that ultimately for Beza, "all theology, even the most technical and scholastic, was pastoral,"[2] Christians studied Scripture and gained theological insights not only to believe what God has revealed; but also to know how God wants persons of faith to live. In times of distress and difficulties, theological beliefs can sustain one's life of faith and provide the comfort and hope one needed.

Our book here seeks to present main features of Theodore Beza's theology. We hope to provide an introductory discussion, a "gateway" to Beza's theological emphases. We have tried to write so those with little, or no, formal theological background will understand Beza's writings. We also hope that those with theological training—pastors, students, or lay persons in churches—will find this book beneficial. A number of technical theological appraisals and studies of Beza have been written. We have not tried to duplicate any of these. Instead, we have wanted to write clearly about what Beza taught. We hope readers will "hear" Beza's voice even as we try to explain what Beza means and why he considered his theological insights to be important for Christian persons in the church. We hope to let Beza speak and we hope to convey what makes Beza's views important today.

We have structured this book by first introducing Beza's life and work so readers can gain a sense of the focuses

1. Wright, *Sovereign*, 14.
2. Wright, *Sovereign*, 84.

and contours of his experience as a Christian and what he tried to do as a church reformer and leader. The chapters that follow focus on theological topics. These are Christian doctrines and emphases that the Christian church—and Beza, as one of its professors/teachers and ministers, considered important. We want to understand what these topics meant for Beza; and what they also mean for us, today. Beza wrote much more than we can consider here. But we hope to have captured and summarized Beza's key insights. We want to understand what Beza thought it was important for Christians to believe and do, then, in his own day, as well as Christians today, in our time. We want, in other words, to allow Beza to be a contemporary contributor to Christian theology as a dialogue partner.

Beza's sixteenth-century context featured the development of Protestant theology and Protestant churches. As a Protestant, Beza's viewpoints stood in distinction from those of Roman Catholicism. On some issues, they contrasted with the emerging Lutheran theological tradition as well as from Anabaptism. As a co-worker with John Calvin, Beza and Calvin shared many viewpoints. In the year of Calvin's death (1564), Beza wrote *Vie de Calvin*, the *Life of Calvin*, to commemorate his friend and colleague whom Beza called his "father in Christ" (*mon pere en Christ*).[3]

Beza believed theology was literally a matter of "life and death." The presence of evil (Satan) in the world was real. In the battle of Satan with God's truth, all persons would be engaged in a spiritual battle, a struggle between salvation, which brings eternal life; and the results of sin, which brings eternal death. Theology matters. Faith matters. Theodore Beza's pastoral theology was to proclaim the gospel of Jesus Christ and the work of salvation in Jesus Christ, carried out by the sovereign God who was the author of salvation and

---

3. See Wright, *Sovereign*, 21.

Lord of all. The Holy Spirit, who brings the gift of faith, witnesses to Jesus Christ, and brings assurance of salvation to Christian believers (Rom 8:16; Gal 4:6).

Beza was passionate that all persons hear the good news of the Christian gospel and come to a true and saving knowledge of Jesus Christ. This "heartbeat" of his theology was made clear in one of his *Household Prayers*, which introduces us to Beza's great concern. Beza prayed for himself—and by extension, for others—to obtain the knowledge of God in Jesus Christ the Savior:

> I beseech thee therefore, my God, vouchsafe, by the light of thy spirit, to address and guide me to the faithful knowledge of this great Savior, whom thou (Father) hast promised from the beginning, and in the latter times revealed, in signs and wonders surpassing all miracles, to the end that being instructed by his doctrine, I may, by him, and in him, know thee to be the eternal living God, and the God of your people, that according to his word I may worship and serve thee in spirit and truth, and in his name call upon thee only in full confidence of your mercy, accompanying him the only subject thereof, and the only mediator of my salvation.[4]

Beza's prayer continues to be important for all, today.

4. Beza, *Prayers*, C5.

1

THEODORE BEZA'S LIFE

INTRODUCTION TO THE LIFE OF BEZA

Preliminary Remarks

WHEN THE NAME OF Beza is known, he is known, generally, by two classes of people. First, he is known by church historians and particularly by students of the Reformation. And second, he is known by New Testament textual critics who are familiar, by virtue of their work, with the Codex named after him, Codex Beza.

The general public, however, is probably unfamiliar with him. The pages that follow are an attempt to correct that situation. Beza was a funny, witty, clever, demanding, articulate, brilliant, and vindictive sixteenth-century theologian. He was the friend of Calvin and his first biographer and he had much of Calvin's temperament about him. But he also had a sharp and acid wit. So, for example, he once remarked, when a man had discovered his wife cheating on him, *in flagrante dilecto,* as it were:

> That official, Ligurinus, whom you discovered
> naked with your wife, wasn't doing anything, I
> swear, except his civic duty; he wanted to evict
> you from public property.[1]

The implication is clear. Ligurinus's wife "got around" and was "public property" and the adulterer was actually doing Ligurinus a favor by freeing him of her. Of course that kind of talk isn't what we usually associate with stodgy and stiff-backed Reformers. And yet there are numerous examples of Beza's racy wit.

The Beza we hope to show readers in the following pages was not only a man of God, he was a man. A totally relatable thoroughly engaging man of varied interests and skills who though silenced and ignored among the majority of Christians at present is very much worth a looking at. We will think together about his life and his theology. We will see him live and we will see him work and we will see him excoriate his enemies and we will see him stand side by side with the greatest of the French Reformers and battle ignorance with him.

BEZA'S EARLY LIFE

Theodore Beza was born in Vézelay, France on the 24th of June, 1519. And Theodore Beza died on October 13, 1605, in Geneva. How he lived, what he did, and what he wrote during the eighty-six years he was a sojourner on planet Earth are the subject of the pages which now follow.[2]

---

1. Citation via Randy Blacketer, *View*, 281.

2. The most extensive and complete English biography of Beza is that of Baird, *Theodore Beza*. Dated, to be sure, and in need of some revision, this remains an amazingly significant work and many of the particulars included here are harvested from Baird's important volume.

Unlike Melanchthon and Luther, along with Calvin and Zwingli, Beza was born no commoner. Indeed, he was of a noble family which carried the name De Besze. Beza is the Latinized version, and when he signed his name Theodore invariably wrote the longer form. History, of course, is never written by the actors themselves but instead is written by those who come later. So while De Besze preferred that form of his name, we know him now as Beza. And that is how he will be referred to throughout.

Beza's home town sits about 150 miles southeast of Paris, as the crow flies. Its greatest claim to fame in Beza's day was that it was the home of a famous Abbey dedicated to Mary Magdalene. Theodore was born on June 24, the Feast day of St. John the Baptist, 1519, to parents Marie and Pierre. Theodore was their seventh child, the third son; and he had four sisters as well.

Shortly after his birth, or at least while still in infancy, Theodore was taken by his uncle (with his parent's permission) to Paris. It is unclear what the uncle saw in the little lad that provoked him to take him to the capital, and it must have taken a toll on Theodore's mother, because she accompanied him to Paris, left him, and died not too long afterward.

The boy had health issues from his earliest days. He was so frail that he didn't learn to walk till almost five years of age and, as Baird notes, physical ailments only worsened from then on.[3] Baird, again, notes,

> At one point in his childhood he became the victim of a malady so painful that he was once, when crossing one of the bridges over the Seine, about to throw himself into the river for the

3. Baird, *Beza*, 6.

purpose of ending his life and his misery in a single moment.[4]

Thankfully the inclination passed and Beza persevered into adolescence and adulthood.

At the ripe old age of nine, circumstances led to his providential (as he himself saw it) placement at a new school for boys in the city of Orléans. He even called the day of his arrival at the school in Orléans his "second birth." It was December 5, 1528. The school at Orléans would become a center of Protestant learning. It was providential indeed that Beza studied there rather than at the University of Paris as his uncle had previously intended.

SCHOOL DAYS

The school in Orléans was the perfect "fit" for a boy of Beza's inclinations, interests, and natural skills. He learned both Latin and Greek so thoroughly that he was easily at home in both as well as he was in his native French. His studies were meaningful to him and they laid the foundation for all his later theological works. But he was not, at the time of his study in Orléans, given to theological pursuits. Poetry seems to have been his first love. And the law.

Curiously, as had been the case in the life of Calvin, Beza seems to have been destined for a career in the law. And, like Calvin, that path was blocked by the God who knows hearts and minds better than the creatures those hearts and minds inhabit. God was, it's probably fair to say, plowing the fertile soil of Beza's intellect to prepare him for a path he had, at the time, no idea he would take. Beza remained in Orléans until 1539 when, Licentiate in Law in hand, he returned to Paris.

4. Baird, *Beza*, 6.

LIFE IN PARIS

When Beza arrived in Paris his interests in both law and theology (which was not then very high up his list of priorities) waned to great extent and he became more engaged in literary pursuits, even going so far as to join himself to the elites of the city and becoming one of their number. Poetry took his attention and held on to it.

From 1539 till 1548 Beza remained in Paris, enjoying life as a man pursuing literature and, it's fair to say, literary fame. He also pursued a woman named Claudine Desnoz whom he married in 1544. Secretly. Though he would marry her in a public ceremony four years later. They would remain married until she died some years afterward.

It was in this period of his life that Beza fell seriously ill and was forced to choose between a life of literary pursuits and a life in service of God. It's intriguing that, in Beza's case, the decision to turn to theological pursuits in service of the faith he embraced in 1548 (the new Evangelical faith) was made not on the basis of a long considered analysis of Calvin's thinking but on the basis of a life-crisis.

As mentioned previously, Beza had been a sickly child and was never a very well man. Illness seems to have been the precipitating event for his theological conversion. Like many in his situation, illness led to a concentrated awareness of God and a serious desire for mercy, followed by a promise of lifelong service if allowed to recover and live. Many people have made the same kind of promise to God. Few follow through on that promise the way Beza did.

Richard Muller observes,

> Two events occurred in 1548 that marked turning points in Beza's life: a book of his Latin poems was published, assuring him some reputation as a literary figure—and, shortly after the book

> appeared, Beza fell gravely ill. The latter experi-
> ence turned him away from his somewhat dis-
> solute existence and appears to have rekindled
> his interest in the reform of the church. Quite
> abruptly, Beza gave up his ecclesiastical income
> and left for Geneva. Once there, he identified
> with the Protestant cause, married Claudine
> (who had been living with him as his mistress),
> and turned his literary skills toward the task of
> reform.[5]

Muller is correct on each point except that Beza never lived with a mistress. As noted above, Beza was married, albeit secretly, to Claudine. And so he arrived in Geneva after recovering from his serious illness and resolving to serve God in the task of reforming the Church. Thus 1548, we can say, was the year of Beza's "conversion" to Reformed belief.

Beza, though, was not yet equipped to carry out the task of Reform because he lacked the one essential skill: Theological training. To be sure, he was a trained Humanist and a man of letters, quite at home in Latin and Greek. But not for the sake of the study of Scripture. Having no background in theological studies to speak of, he first had to take that task in hand. It was in that condition that he met John Calvin.

BEZA IN LAUSANNE

Beza arrived in Geneva and was warmly welcomed by Calvin, who was happy to see the young man he had met earlier in life. But Beza was there only a short time before he went north to Germany to visit with his old professor, Melchior Wolmar, who was by then in Tübingen. Realizing that he could not remain in Germany, Beza decided to return to

5. Muller, *Reformation Theologians*, 214.

Geneva but along the way, passing through Lausanne, met Pierre Viret, who was then busy assembling a faculty for the newly established University of Lausanne. Beza's learning being well enough known to Viret, he offered the traveler a chair at the university. Beza hesitated, even continuing his journey to Geneva where he consulted Calvin and others on the matter. He was eventually persuaded that this was the calling of God and he assumed the Chair in Sacred and Secular Learning.

> Thus began the course of a brilliant and fruitful professorship extending over a period of nine years, 1549–1558. The work was congenial. All his past studies had prepared Theodore Beza for a thorough discharge of its duties. Greek was his favourite tongue. Its direct bearing upon the preparation for the Christian ministry of the youth that were drawn to his class-room by the reputation of his learning, procured him peculiar gratification.[6]

It was here, in Lausanne, during his years as a teacher of Greek, that Beza honed his theological skills through extensive discussions with colleagues and friends and students. Like Karl Barth much later, Beza became the theologian he became in the crucible of teaching.

It was while in Lausanne that Beza turned from writing poetry (which he had done with delight as a young man) to writing theological treatises. His first, composed in 1554, and titled *Treatise on the Punishment of Heretics*, in the wake of the execution for heresy of Michael Servetus, was brutal. Schaff opined:

> The book has a polemic and an apologetic part.
> In the former, Beza tries to refute the principle

6. Baird, *Beza*, 48.

of toleration; in the latter, to defend the conduct of Geneva. He contends that the toleration of error is indifference to truth, and that it destroys all order and discipline in the Church.

When heresy is confirmed, the State must

proceed after quiet, regular examination of the heresy and mature consideration of all the circumstances, and inflict such punishment as will best secure the honor due to the divine Majesty and the peace and unity of the Church.

If that meant killing the heretics, Beza would argue, so be it. This would be a bridge too far for Schaff, who remarked:

This theory, which differs little from the papal theory of intolerance, except in regard to the definition of heresy and the mode and degree of punishment, was accepted for a long time in the Reformed Churches with few dissenting voices; but, fortunately, there was no occasion for another capital punishment of heresy in the Church of Geneva after the burning of Servetus. The evil which Calvin and Beza did was buried with their bones; the greater good which they did will live on forever.[7]

The importance of this book is hard to overstate. Not because of its tone or intention, but because it shows Beza to be a man of incredibly decided opinions and a man unwilling to deviate from his views once those views have, in his mind, received scriptural justification. Or perhaps to state it differently, once Beza had made up his mind on a theological issue, that was where he stayed. In that respect he was very much like Calvin. It is thus easy to see why

7. This and the citations above, from Schaff, *History*, vol. 8.

the two men would later get along so famously and so harmoniously.

Yet even a historian as admiring of Beza as his biographer Henry Martyn Baird cannot stomach the Reformer's attitudes as revealed in his first theological tome. Baird writes:

> Most deplorable indeed is the error of Beza, both because of the perverted view he presented of the duty of the Christian Church to appeal to the State for aid in its conflict with heresy, and because of the equally disastrous notion he entertained of the duty of the Christian ruler to punish, even with death, the crime of active dissent from the Church's tenets.[8]

Even the greatest people are chained to their own day. But writing against heretics and for their punishment would not be the only thing Beza did in Lausanne. He would also become the spokesman for the Reformed faith wherever and whenever the opportunity presented itself. When persecution broke out, Beza spoke up. He was a defender of the faith with the same zeal with which he was the condemner of heretics like Servetus. He even went so far as to journey to Germany to assist Reformed believers in their troubles.

Yet outsiders to the Reformed faith were not his only concern during these years. Like Bucer, he wanted very much to bring the Protestants and Reformed together. Particularly in regards to their teachings on the Supper. And like Bucer, he failed to do so. But whereas Bucer had a more conciliatory disposition, Beza was driven by a sense of rightness which, naturally, doomed his efforts from the start. Compromise was not his strong suit.

8. Baird, *Beza*, 69.

BEZA RETURNS TO GENEVA

In 1558 Beza resigned his position at Lausanne and returned to Geneva to take up a post at the soon to be established (by Calvin) university. Established, then, in 1559, Beza was appointed rector of the University of Geneva, or as it was named then, the Schola Genevensis. Naturally his duties also included teaching Greek.

Excursus: The University of Geneva

> The university was founded in 1559 as the Academy of Geneva (Académie de Genève) by John Calvin, as a seminary administrated by the Company of Pastors, to be the center of public education in Protestant Geneva. With the goal of educating not only pastors but also magistrates for the republic, in 1565 the academy began the teaching of Law.
>
> During the French annexation of Geneva (1798–1813), the school was reorganized into a more universal format, with the introduction of degrees and its division in faculties. This process of modernization continued into the period of national Restoration.[9]

Upon his return to Geneva and his appointment as rector and professor of Greek, Beza set out to carry out his responsibilities as vigorously as possible. As Karin Maag notes:

> In his inauguration address on 5 June 1559, Beza highlighted the biblical roots of the Genevan emphasis on education, and the distinctiveness

9. Wikipedia, "University of Geneva," https://en.wikipedia.org/wiki/University_of_Geneva#History.

of the academy, where young men would put
their learning in the service of God.[10]

Nothing clearer nor more precise could describe the work
of Beza in Geneva than his striving to help young men put
their learning in the service of God. He would spend the
remainder of his life doing exactly that.

RETURN TO FRANCE

Events in France about the same time that the University
of Geneva was "getting off the ground" meant a change in
the plans of Beza, who was involved in attempts to help
Reformed believers find peaceful existence in his home-
land. Invited by them to return to France, he did so, with
the blessing of Geneva, who granted him a leave of absence
in 1561. The period of his sojourn in France lasted from
1561 till 1563. He there participated in a number of public
debates and discussions even while France was being torn
apart by religious warfare. While intriguing and important, and brilliantly described by Baird in his impressive
biography,[11] the details of this segment of Beza's life cannot
detain us further. He returned to Geneva in 1563 and that
is where we next turn.

THE RETURN TO GENEVA AND
CONTINUATION OF HIS WORK

Beza's two year absence from Geneva, while important to
him and to the cause of the Reformation in France, was
something of an interruption to his primary tasks: to teach
Greek and to help his students become the ministers of God

10. Maag, *Expository Times*, 264.
11. Baird, *Beza*, chs. 7–12.

that God wished them to be. Beza arrived back in Geneva on May 5, 1563, to a joyful populace. They were glad to see him! But joy soon found itself replaced by sorrow because just over a year after his return, John Calvin died (May 27, 1564).

It fell to Beza to write the life story of Calvin and to continue the work of the Reformer just as it fell to Bullinger to carry on the work of Zwingli when the latter perished on the field as chaplain to the troops of Zurich at the Second Battle of Kappel-am-Albis on October 11, 1531. Beza had, as it were, massive shoes to fill. And he did not disappoint.

Indeed, within a year he had produced his own edition of the Greek New Testament. In 1565 he published the Greek text accompanied by two columns of Latin text. The first was the Vulgate, and the second was Beza's own translation of the Greek text into Latin. Beza's Greek text was a scantily revised copy of Stephanus's 1551 Greek New Testament along with, as mentioned above, two columns of Latin. Beza's chief contribution to the edition being, again, his own translation in Latin of the Greek of Stephanus. Beza's first edition is available on the internet at E-Rara.[12] It would appear in five editions in total, being published in 1556/1557, 1565, 1582, 1588, and finally 1598. It exerted immense influence and was used by Reformed theologians and biblical scholars for decades, serving as the basis for both the Geneva Bible and the King James Version. The Greek text which Beza utilized for his edition was donated by him in 1581 to the University of Cambridge and there came to be called Codex Bezae (D). It contains the Gospels and the book of Acts in a bilingual Greek and Latin edition.

12. See E-Rara, https://www.e-rara.ch/gep_g/doi/10.3931/e-rara -6094.

(*A portion of Mark 5 in D. Photo in the public domain*)

But editions of the New Testament are not the only works that Beza published in his productive Geneva years. He wrote on topics as varied as the Lord's Supper, Heresies, Confessions, a tragedy in French on Abraham, orations, letters, a biography of Calvin, tractates on divorce and polygamy, on the Trinity, and many others. Some of which we will encounter again in the chapters to follow when we look more carefully into Beza's theology.

BEZA AND THE ENGLISH REFORMATION

As had been the case in the life of Martin Bucer, Theodore Beza too had an international reach. Previously his assistance rendered to Reformed communities in France has been mentioned.[13] He also rendered aid to the Reformed in Britain.

When the vestment controversy broke out in England after Elizabeth I replaced Queen Mary, the clergy sought guidance from their colleagues in Switzerland. Notably, they asked Bullinger and Beza their advice. Beza was

13. We leave aside his further assistance to the French brethren after the Saint Bartholomew's day Massacre, concerning which see Baird.

disinclined to urge clerics to leave the ministry for such a trivial reason as the clothing they were required, or not, to wear. Indeed, when the controversy heated up Bullinger wrote to Beza intimating that

> it was now their decided resolution to have nothing more to do with anyone in this controversy, whether in conversation or by letter. "And if any other parties think of coming hither," they added, "let them know that they will come to no purpose."[14]

Bullinger simply had no interest at all in being dragged further into English squabbles. Beza, on the other hand, was younger and more inclined to enter the fray the longer it dragged on. When Elizabeth made demands of the clerics it was too much for Beza to bear and he struck. The queen's demands needn't be submitted to.

So on June 27, 1566, he wrote a very long letter to Bishop Grindal in which he elevated doctrine over ritual and urged Grindal to take the same course. Ritual mattered very little when it had no doctrinal basis. Beza's views on the topic are, in a word, very Reformed:

> The letter ended with some stinging words of rebuke for those who wished to force the ministers to pledge themselves to obey whatever the queen and the bishops might hereafter prescribe in matters of ecclesiastical ritual.[15]

It was easy for Beza to urge such boldness since it wouldn't be his head Elizabeth separated from his body if she were aggrieved by his rebellious actions and words. However the issue turned out, though, a new phase in Beza's life was about to begin. He would become a controversialist.

14. Baird, *Beza*, 259.
15. Baird, *Beza*, 262.

BEZA THE CONTROVERSIALIST

The investiture controversy was not Beza's first (recall his stance on Servetus and the treatment of heretics) and it would not be his last. Indeed, it seems to have set him on a course of controversy which he traveled for the rest of his life. Polemics became his forte. Particularly in matters concerning election, providence, and the Supper. The materials related to these subjects are collected in his *Theological Treatises* of 1582 in two large Latin volumes of, respectively, 694 pages and 363 pages.

BEZA AND THE SINGING OF PSALMS

While widely known as the friend and colleague of John Calvin and the sometimes rather harsh controversialist as well as the textual critic, Beza was also involved in very significant ways of organizing the liturgy and providing a Psalter for the Reformed Christians in France; the so-called Huguenots. Baird goes so far as to claim that "now the French psalms were peculiarly the work of Theodore Beza."[16] And while the work of Clement Marot is noteworthy, Baird insists that the Psalter used in Reformed worship in France was Beza's.

The Psalter was not merely a songbook though. In the sixteenth century the singing of the Psalms in a church service was viewed by both the Roman Catholic Church and the government of France as a marker of a congregation of heretics. Indeed, something so commonly taken for granted today as singing in church, was forbidden then. Baird notes:

> Up to this date the psalms in the vernacular had
> been almost uniformly proscribed by Church

16. Baird, *Beza*, 288.

and State. The singing of them by the common people was taken as a sure sign of heresy.[17]

The attitude of the French court shifted in the early 1560s, though, due to relative popularity in the court itself for the tunes to which the Psalms were being set, and in 1561 Beza and Marot's edition of the metrical Psalter was published with a royal license thanks to the newly issued Edict of January which permitted such publications. Worth repeating in its entirety is Baird's observations concerning the importance of this Edict permitting Psalter publications:

> Beza secured for the complete psalter translated by Clement Marot and himself a privilege, or governmental authorisation and copyright. The date of its issue was December 26, 1561. And now began a very deluge of editions of the psalter following one another almost without intermission. Such was the new and quickened demand, that it was difficult, almost impossible, to keep up with it. Besides other issues which have undoubtedly escaped notice, we know of twenty-five or twenty-six distinct editions that were put out within the bounds of the single year 1562; that is, a distinct edition on the average for every fortnight.[18]

It is extraordinary that such a deluge of Psalters were unleashed by the end of 1562 and it demonstrates both the popularity of song books and congregational singing in worship. Beza's least known contribution turns out to be, in practical terms, his most important and his longest lasting. Baird agrees, and goes further, writing:

17. Baird, *Beza*, 299.
18. Baird, *Beza*, 303.

That the Reformed religion gained ground in no slight extent from the stress that was laid upon psalm-singing, is a fact that cannot be ignored ; nor can it be denied that the psalms themselves owed much of their power to the suitable and attractive music to which they were set.[19]

Theodore Beza, theologian, also contributed to liturgical practices and to practical issues like the singing of Psalms in the church's worship. Time fails to relate the further contributions of Beza in the field of historical research, and his work as a patriotic preacher, bolstering his nation's political and economic systems, and his other accomplishments. We now turn to the last years of his life in Geneva.

BEZA'S FINAL YEARS

It was noted earlier in this brief biography that Beza was never a very well man. Illnesses dogged him his entire life. The last quarter of his time on earth saw ever declining health. Though impaired, his work was not halted and he devoted his time to a final revision of the French Bible and offering his very well attended lectures on the Bible and theological matters. Indeed, he was immensely popular. Baird observes:

> Beza was the first citizen of Geneva, the man who was always at his post, however it might be with others, the one man whom everybody went to see on arriving, and again before his departure. No student was well satisfied with himself unless he took away a letter of commendation from the old patriarch, or, at the very least, an album in which was inscribed his characteristic

19. Baird, *Beza*, 304.

signature with some verses kindly composed for the occasion.[20]

Beza was beloved. And when he died, the city mourned, along with all of the people of France who were adherents of the Reformed faith. His fellow clerics visited him in pairs every day for the last months of his life, encouraging him to remain steadfast in faith and to think of the coming reward in glory he was sure to receive.

The day of his death, October 13, 1605, was a Sunday. He awakened that morning feeling refreshed and improved. He was able to take a few steps and to eat a few bites of food. And then he asked a question:

> "Is the city in full safety and quiet?" he asked. Then, on receiving an affirmative answer, he suddenly sank down, losing strength and consciousness at once, and in a few minutes passed peacefully away, while sorrowing friends prayed about his bedside.[21]

Though rather long, the notice published following Beza's death is worth repeating in its entirety:

> What the haven is to those that sail, that is the removal into another life to those whose death is precious in the eyes of the Lord. Inasmuch, therefore, as yesterday that great light of the Church, that reverend man, Doctor Theodore Beza, worn out with years, was peacefully translated from this transitory and wretched life to that other life in which there is eternal blessedness free from disquietude, and inasmuch as he is this day to be consigned to burial, the illustrious and generous lords, counts, barons, nobles,

20. Baird, *Beza*, 331–32.
21. Baird, *Beza*, 350.

all in fine that apply themselves to letters now present in this Academy, are invited, in the name of the Pastors and Professors, to-day at noon, to pay this last honour due to so great a man and one that has died in so pious a manner, and to attend his funeral. Whose body indeed, like as the bodies of all that die in Christ, is sown in corruption, but shall be raised in incorruption : in such wise that neither death nor life shall separate us from the love which is in Jesus Christ our Lord, who translates His children from death to life. He died on the thirteenth of October, 1605.[22]

How are we to understand Theodore Beza? As a man, he lived a life of ill health and struggled to achieve everything he achieved. As a theologian, he contributed to the life of the church in important ways. As a friend, he left a deep impression on all who knew him, endearing himself to them by being the kind of friend everyone should have. To his foes, he was inimitable, brash, brusque, and sometimes even abusive. But seldom was he wrong. He is not as well known as Luther or Melanchthon or Calvin or Bullinger or Bucer or Zwingli, but he is no less important than them and his influence on the French Reformed tradition exceeds them all save Calvin himself.

QUESTIONS FOR DISCUSSION

1. How do you think Beza's illnesses affected his work?

2. Do you think that Beza's Psalter was as influential as Baird suggests?

---

22. Baird, *Beza*, 351.

3. Why do you think Beza is less well known than the
   other Reformers?

4. What is the most important aspect of Beza's legacy to
   you?

2

THE DOCTRINE OF GOD

BEZA'S DOCTRINE OF GOD

THEODORE BEZA WAS A theologically conservative Reformed Christian. His understanding of God, who God is, what God does, how God acts, how God manifests himself, and everything to do with God aligned with Calvin and Bullinger and Zwingli and Luther and other Protestant and Reformed Christians' views.

This view of God was nicely summarized in the so-called Apostles' Creed, which states:

> I believe in God, the Father almighty, creator of heaven and earth.
>
> I believe in Jesus Christ, his only Son, our Lord, who was conceived by the Holy Spirit and born of the virgin Mary. He suffered under Pontius Pilate, was crucified, died, and was buried; he descended to hell. The third day he rose again from the dead. He ascended to heaven and is seated at the right hand of God the Father

almighty. From there he will come to judge the living and the dead.

I believe in the Holy Spirit, the holy catholic church, the communion of saints, the forgiveness of sins, the resurrection of the body, and the life everlasting. Amen.

God is Father, Son, and Holy Spirit. God is creator, redeemer, and sustainer. These theological claims would have seemed not only sensible to the Reformers (and among their number, Beza) but true. Absolute truth.

Nonetheless it is very much worth noting that Beza's *explanation* of the Doctrine of God is important and worthy of consideration. He may have believed what others believed but his *expression* of that belief is remarkably engaging.

And while it is true, as Genton notes, that Beza

> devoted his entire life to using all the means at his disposal to at the very least sustain and, at best, to propagate the theological and organizational legacy of Calvin. He defended the Reformed doctrine when it was attacked; and explicated Reformed doctrine through lectures. He used all literary genres available to do this: theater, poetry, debate, satire, treatise, letter, translation.[1]

It is also true, again, and this cannot be stated too frequently, that in many ways Beza was his own man theologically, as we shall see throughout, including in his exposition of the doctrine of God.

Beza described who God is and what God does in his brilliantly formulated Catechism. This catechism, designed for children, is important precisely because it makes the very notion of Deity comprehensible to young people. This

1. Genton, *Companion*, 117.

is no small accomplishment. Accordingly, what follows will be drawn chiefly from Beza's little booklet titled *A Book of Christian Questions and Answers*.[2] The book came to life in a very productive period of Beza's theological works. As Richard Muller notes, correctly:

> The decade following 1570 was an era of considerable literary activity on Beza's part. He devoted considerable energy to the edition of his major theological essays in the three volumes of his Tractationes theologicae, which appeared between 1570 and 1582. In addition, he also wrote his expanded catechesis, the two-part *Quaestionum & responsionum christianarum libellus*, during this time.[3]

BEZA'S CATECHISM

Who is God? What is God like? Beza avoids speculations concerning the being or inner nature of God because these notions have no ground in Scripture. Instead, Beza (and in his catechism) takes for granted first of all the existence of God. God is. There is no question about that. God exists and is present and active in the world and in the life of those who believe. God is the God who acts. The God who does. The God who engages with his creation and loves it.

2. This little volume was published in 1572. The publisher, Hugh Singleton of London, notes that the booklet was written in Latin and translated by Arthur Golding. The extracts from this volume in this chapter are provided in modernized English by the present author. The English of 1572 needed to be updated. However, the booklet contains no pagination. This is not a serious problem since the citations which are drawn from it are easily traceable for anyone interested in seeing the whole since the booklet is not large.

3. Lindberg, *Reformation Theologians*, 216.

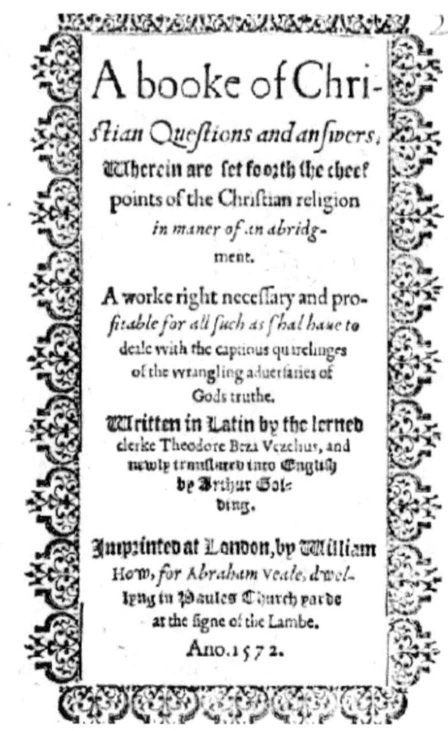

Title page of the 1527 Book of Christian Questions and Answers

The catechism begins with this notion of God as its unstated premise. The questions and answers, unlike the case of the Heidelberg Catechism, are not numbered. The opening Question asks and answers, "Who has set us in the world? Answer: God, of his own singular goodness." And this is followed by the question "To What end?" This is answered, "To the end that we should serve him: and that he should be glorified by giving us eternal life."

God has created humankind for two purposes: to know him and to serve him. If this reminds readers of the opening of Calvin's *Institutes*, it should. Calvin influenced

Beza as much as he influenced all those who gathered around him both as colleagues and congregants. Calvin's magnum opus begins similarly with its "Our wisdom, in so far as it ought to be deemed true and solid Wisdom, consists almost entirely of two parts: the knowledge of God and of ourselves" (*Inst* 1.1.1). In Beza's mind knowing God and ourselves means knowing God and serving him. Or, knowing that we are servants of God.

Beza believed that people exist to serve God and their lives are fulfilled or lived to the fullest when they see themselves as living to serve the Lord. The purpose of life, for Beza, is to serve God fully. Any life lived which falls short of service of God is a life lived poorly. Theology, or our understanding of God, must issue in proper behavior. Knowing God means knowing God must be served.

Keeping in mind that Beza is constructing his catechism for children, the primary aim of his questions and answers is to help youngsters understand not only God, but themselves. His is not a theology divorced from daily life. Indeed, every step along the way is a reminder to readers how life is to be lived. Beza would disdain speculative theology which only has as its goal a thinking about God. God must be thought about in order for the thinker to live a life pleasing to God.

Since worship was critically important in the sixteenth century, and was nothing less than the center and organizing principle of both the sacred and the secular, it is noteworthy that Beza's next catechetical question has to do with the act of worship. He asks, "Which is the way to worship him aright, and consequently to attain eternal life and to glorify him properly?" The answer: "To know and acknowledge him after the same manner that he has disclosed himself to us in his Word."

God, for Beza, was the object of worship and the only proper object of adoration for Christians. It is only in proper worship that people are able to "attain" everlasting life. Does this suggest that for Beza it is the act of worship that "saves"? No. As he will spell out further in the questions and answers which follow, God gives everlasting life to those who know and love him. Rather, worship is the place and occasion where God is made known. Everlasting life is the gift of God which implies that for Beza God is the God who gives.

Worship, then, has to do with the reception of God and God's provision primarily of salvation but also of every good and perfect gift. This aspect of Beza's theology will be worked out further in the chapter on worship in this volume. The point here is that the discussion of the doctrine of God, for Beza, meant the discussion of worship. God and worship are inseparable as are worship and God. There is no Christian faith without God. Nor is there Christian faith without worship.

But how is this God known? If God is the maker of us and the world and we are made to serve him everlastingly, how are we to come to know these things? What is the source of these truths and where may they be found? The catechism moves next to ask and answer precisely these questions.

"What do you call the Word of God?" And the answer: "That which the Prophets and Apostles received from God's Spirit and committed to writing, which books we call the Old and the New Testament." This, of course, raises a number of important questions. Why does Beza see the word of God as the Scriptures rather than as Jesus? He obviously affirms "inspiration" but does he mean thereby literal word for word verbal inspiration via dictation or something more general? These issues will be investigated in the chapter on

Scripture in the following chapter. Here it is important to note that what we know of God we know only through Scripture. Scripture is the place where God reveals himself.

Beza offers a bit of insight into his understanding of Scripture in the question and answer which follow: "Who then is the author of those books?" Answer: "God himself, through the pens of the Prophets and Apostles." God dictated, the prophets and apostles wrote. Beza, then, appears to base his theology of God (and the other doctrines which he explains in his catechism) on plenary verbal inspiration. This is an important aspect of Beza's theology because it will become incredibly influential in various corners of Reformed theology and especially in the branch of Reformed Christianity known as Evangelical Fundamentalism. Yet, importantly, it would be a mistake to see Beza as a "Fundamentalist." It would first be anachronistic, as Fundamentalism was not a movement within Christianity until its birth in the early 1900s. And second it would be unfair. Conservatism in theology is not the same as Fundamentalism.

The significance of Scripture in connection with the doctrine of God in the theology of Beza lies in the fact that without Scripture God simply cannot be rightly known nor rightly served. People would be left adrift were Scripture absent; and Scripture would be without authority were God not its author. There is, then, for Beza, a very practical reason for his view of the inspiration of Scripture. All of which will be developed more further in our chapter below regarding Scripture. For now it will suffice to make the main point that Beza will spend the next several questions and answers in his Catechism on the topic of the whence of Scripture.

God for Beza, as for all of the other Reformers of the first and second generation, asserted that God made himself known in and through Scripture as the Triune God.

Beza affirmed that God is the Trinity. "These three persons, then, are they three gods in the same way that three men are three beings?" asks Beza.

Answer: "These three persons are not separated from one another, but only distinguished from one another. So, just as the Father is not the Son or the Holy Spirit, but only the Father, nor the Son the Father or the Holy Spirit, but only the Son, nor the Holy Spirit the Father or the Son but only the Holy Spirit. Yet all of those several persons are one selfsame perfect God; everlasting, of one essence, perfectly equal."

Beza's attempt to explain the Trinity as part of his theology of God crashes on the same rock that all such attempts crash. The Trinity is incomprehensible mystery and every attempt to describe it results in inaccuracies. To be sure, Beza knows that this doctrine is mystery and says as much in the question and answer which immediately follow the preceding.

Beza's treatment of the Trinity, then, like his other expositions of key theological themes, is "orthodox" in the sense of well and widely received among Western Christians. He continues to describe the persons of the Trinity and their functions as his Catechism continues to unveil the central teachings of the Christian faith. Beza's genius lies not so much in his explanations, but in his ability to weave the whole together seamlessly. His gift is coherence.

Moving forward from the mystery of the Trinity he turns next to the doctrine of salvation which he also subsumes under the general doctrine of God. Every doctrine, it seems, is for Beza a subset of the doctrine of God. God is the large category into which must be fit the doctrine of Scripture, the Trinity, Salvation, and the rest to come. These doctrines are impossible to disentangle from the doctrine of God himself. This has the consequence of our own having to separate what Beza doesn't separate. We must treat the various doctrines in a somewhat independent way while Beza himself never attempted to "divide the baby"; being too wise for that as was Solomon before him.

Investigating, then, God's salvific work, Beza asks, "Is knowledge of God's essence sufficient to save a man?" This is an excellent question. Does knowing various facts about God result in salvation itself? Does affirming these facts "save" a person? This may be the most important question Beza asks and answers as it gets to the very core of what authentic salvation "requires" of a person. Does our agreement with doctrinal assertions result in our redemption, or is something else going on in salvation as act? This is the heart of Beza's concern.

His answer to his own question is telling: "No . . . what we must know most of all is what God thinks of us." What then is the most important thing to know about God? Beza's answer is incredibly brief: "Perfect justice and perfect mercy."

God's chief attributes are not, in Beza's catechism, omnipotence, omnipresence, omniscience, or any of the other aspects of the being of God. Not even love is listed as the most important or meaningful part of the being of God. To be sure love is an aspect of God's being, but it is subsumed under the twin foci of justice and mercy.

But does Beza believe that these things are "qualities" of God's being or essence? No. "These things are not in God, as qualities. But by God's justice I mean that God's nature is so pure and sound of itself the he utterly hates and most severely punishes all unrighteousness."

God's nature and God's "qualities" are different things in Beza's thinking. It is one of the most intriguing aspects of Beza's thinking that he sees a distinction between "nature" and "quality." This stems from his philosophical understanding and though telling, it is not helpful. Beza here makes a distinction without a difference. It is, however, an important example of the fact that when philosophy intrudes into theology, confusion erupts. And Beza, like the other first- and second-generation Reformers, had more than a little training in and understanding of philosophy, which naturally had an impact on their theological presentations and, more importantly, their underlying conceptions of God.

As Shawn Wright astutely observes,

> Brian Armstrong, an historian of the French Reformation, critiques Beza specifically for his theological method because he abandoned Calvin's careful biblical method. In its place Beza erected speculation. Beza's scholastic theological method, according to Armstrong, "represents a profound divergence from the humanistically oriented religion of John Calvin and most of the early reformers. The strongly biblically and experientially based theology of Calvin and Luther had, it is fair to say, been overcome by the metaphysics and deductive logic of a restored Aristotelianism."[4]

Beza's chief departure from Calvin is, indeed, methodological.

And what does Beza understand by "the mercy of God"? "I mean that whatever God gives us (especially everlasting life) proceeds completely from his free gift of grace." How, then, can Beza balance the justice of God and the mercy of God? This question has been an important one since at least the composition of the book of Job. How can God, who is just, allow injustice and how does that align with the notion that God is merciful? What is merciful about a house crashing in on all of Job's children and killing

4. Wright, *Man and the Myth*, 33.

them instantly? And what injustice had been done to merit such punishment? Indeed, if God punishes injustice, why does injustice exist for very long at all? And if God is merciful, why do awful things continue to happen? These are the issues which attach themselves to the question at hand in Beza's catechism: how is God both just and merciful?

Beza answers, "These things (justice and mercy) do very well agree; the Father has freely given the Son who has made full satisfaction for our sins." Few will see that as a very helpful answer, but it is the answer provided by Beza and it must have been sufficient for him since Beza immediately turns away from the thorny problem to discuss the doctrine of the atonement and the death of Jesus.

As this will be covered more fully in another chapter in this volume, at present, because it is closely connected to the doctrine of God, here only the highlights of Beza's understanding of the atonement will be described. Remembering that every doctrine has its center in God and the exposition of every doctrine eventually leads back to and centers in God.

The central question for Beza is: Why did Jesus have to die for our sins? Couldn't God have saved us by another means? He certainly could, says Beza, but "this was the most convenient means for God to show both his absolute justice and his absolute mercy." Jesus had to die for our sins because, in the plan of God, this was the clearest way God could show humanity both his perfect justice and his perfect mercy. If he had saved us without satisfying the penalty of sin he would not be just, and if he did not save us at all he would not be merciful.

Beza's doctrine is incredibly insightful if examined in its details. God is merciful. God is just. Sin is part and parcel of the human experience. What is God to do? If he simply "forgives sin" with the wave of his hand or the utterance of his mouth then he shows himself to have very little concern for justice. How, after all, could a just God simply ignore sin and its exceptional dire consequences for human beings? Sin's destructive power would be ignored. And sin's impact on the lives of its victims would be overlooked. Justice demands otherwise.

Scriptures are packed with references to the justice of God. Perhaps the most telling is found in Genesis, in the story of Abraham's discussion with God regarding the people of Sodom and Gomorrah:

> And Abraham came near and said, "Would You also destroy the righteous with the wicked? Suppose there were fifty righteous within the city; would You also destroy the place and not spare it for the fifty righteous that were in it? "Far be it from You to do such a thing as this, to slay the righteous with the wicked, so that the righteous should be as the wicked; far be it from You! Shall not the Judge of all the earth do justice?" So the LORD said, "If I find in Sodom fifty righteous within the city, then I will spare all the place for their sakes." Then Abraham answered and said, "Indeed now, I who am but dust and ashes have taken it upon myself to speak to the Lord: Suppose there were five less than the fifty righteous; would You destroy all of the city for lack of five?" So He said, "If I find there forty-five, I will not destroy it." And he spoke to Him yet again and said, "Suppose there should be forty found there?" So He said, "I will not do it for the sake of forty." Then he said, "Let not the Lord be angry, and I will speak: Suppose thirty should be found there?" So He said, "I will not do it if I find thirty there." And he said, "Indeed now, I have taken it upon myself to speak to the Lord: Suppose twenty should be found there?" So He

> said, "I will not destroy it for the sake of twenty."
> Then he said, "Let not the Lord be angry, and I
> will speak but once more: Suppose ten should be
> found there?" And He said, "I will not destroy
> it for the sake of ten." So the LORD went His
> way as soon as He had finished speaking with
> Abraham; and Abraham returned to his place.
> (Gen 18:23–33 NKJV)

Scripture is clear—God must do what is right. It is who he is.

But if God does not find some means of providing forgiveness, then how can he be described as merciful? Mercy is one of the characteristics of God which both the Scriptures of the Old and New Testaments have reiterated numerous times. Indeed, in the New King James Version, the word "mercy" occurs 282 times. One example should suffice:

> Have mercy on me, O LORD, for I am in trouble;
> My eye wastes away with grief, Yes, my soul and
> my body! For my life is spent with grief, And my
> years with sighing; My strength fails because of
> my iniquity, And my bones waste away. I am a
> reproach among all my enemies, But especially
> among my neighbors, And am repulsive to my
> acquaintances; Those who see me outside flee
> from me. I am forgotten like a dead man, out
> of mind; I am like a broken vessel. For I hear
> the slander of many; Fear is on every side; While
> they take counsel together against me, They
> scheme to take away my life. But as for me, I
> trust in You, O LORD; I say, "You are my God."
> (Ps 31:9–14 NKJV)

Mercy is one of God's key attributes because it is the motive by which he operates in order to offer forgiveness and to, frankly, make the lives of sinners better.

So, to return again to Beza's claim that the atonement of Jesus was the best way for God to show both his justice and his mercy; when taken seriously both the justice of God and the mercy of God must be operative. But how? By allowing Jesus to die in the place of all the sinners who deserved death—thus taking full account of the justice of God and the mercy of God simultaneously, in one simple singular act. It seems that no other theories of the atonement were sufficient for Beza.

The nature of Christ is next up in Beza's catechism but we will leave this issue aside until we arrive at the discussion of the Doctrine of Christ. The catechism, in fact, spends many pages discussing the meaning of Christ's imputed righteousness, why it is necessary, and what it means for believers. It would not be an exaggeration to say that Christ is the center of Beza's catechism and that he spends more effort and energy describing the work of Christ than either the work of the Father or the work of the Holy Spirit.

Beza's *Brief and Pithy Summary of the Christian Faith*

What other sources, then, might we consult in which Beza discusses his understanding of God? We can find his understanding of God in section 1 of his *Brief and Pithy Summary of the Christian Faith*, translated by Robert Fyll from French and published in London around 1566 (the date is not certain and it isn't included on the printer's title page). As is the case of so many books published in the sixteenth century, there are no page numbers on the pages of books. The printer of the present volume, though, does provide a section-by-section listing of the contents of the book and the folios on which those contents of those books appear. The volume follows the order of the Apostles' Creed and, accordingly, comes to the doctrine of God on the first pages.

> We believe that there is only one divine sub-
> stance, which we call God, and that not only
> because the contemplation of natural things
> teaches us to do so, but mostly because the Holy
> Scriptures bear witness to Him.[5]

Beza believed God revealed himself not only in Scripture but in nature. Scripture was the primary source of our
knowledge of God, but nature itself also pointed to God.
The existence of grass and trees and rabbits and water and
deer and flowers and men and women and stars and the
sun and the moon and everything else point to a maker,
a creator, a cause. Beza knew that cause to be God. And
more importantly, Beza was of the opinion that anyone else
looking at everything around him or her would also assume a Creator. Who this Creator was, what he was named,
what he was like cannot, though, be seen in nature itself.
Instead, that Creator must reveal himself and he does that
in Scripture.

Then follows, in the summary, in order, discussions
of the Trinity, the Father's nature, the Father as Creator and
Preserver of creation, the Angels (who are servants of the
Father), the Father as made known in the Son, the mercy and
grace of the Father, the creation of mankind, their fall and
their continuation in sin, and the solution of the problem of
sin in Christ. This, naturally, leads to the consideration of
the second article of the Creed. There is nothing in these ar-
ticulations of the faith that differ substantially or materially
from the material found in the Catechism, discussed above.

Beza, then, maintained theological positions that were
fairly consistent throughout. What he asserts in the *Summary* in 1566 he maintains in the mid 1570s and later.

5. Beza, *Brief and Pithy*, n.p.

Beza's Propositions and Principles of Divinity[6]

Perhaps the most systematic of Beza's presentations of the loci of theology, this lengthy work (it's 425 pages long) discusses virtually every doctrine including but not limited to God, the Trinity, good works, election, predestination, the sacraments, and the rest. It also includes an exposition of the Commandments and the Lord's Prayer, and sections on the Ministry and the State. It is a full and rich exemplar of Beza's grasp of every theological doctrine.

The first three pages are where Beza's discussion of the doctrine of God are found. He begins as he did in the Catechism; with a reminder that true knowledge of God is the aim of life but then he goes on to note that since this is the case, people should spend their lives in seeking to know the God whom we must know.

Of course a full and perfect knowledge of God can never be achieved by human beings, or even angels, still we should "bend all the powers of our souls and bodies to know God."[7] This knowledge of God is derived from contemplation of the works and power of God. We know what we know about God, in other words, by what God does and how God does it.

The remainder of the exposition of the doctrine of God in this particular volume of Beza's follows what we also learn from the catechism and his other works. Here, however, we have a more academic orientation of presentation. The Catechism and the *Pithy Summary* are aimed at the young and the general public (if I may be permitted

6. *Propositions and Principles of Divinity* was originally published in Latin but here appears in a translated edition in English, in 1595. It purports to be the "minutes" of a debate held between students at the University of Geneva under the guidance of Beza.

7. Beza, *Propositions*, 4. Unlike so many volumes from this period, this one is paginated.

such a descriptor). But the *Propositions and Principles* has budding theologians in its sights and as a consequence in many of the chapters to follow this exquisite work will be the basis of our understanding of Beza's theology.

Indeed, in the remaining pages of this volume, the particulars of Beza's interpretation of Jesus, the Holy Spirit, sin and salvation, the church and its ministries, the Word and the sacraments, and the state and the last things will all be considered. At the end we will ask whether or not Beza continues to be important. To "matter."

QUESTIONS FOR DISCUSSION

1. How does Beza's understanding of God affect your understanding of God?

2. Do you find yourself agreeing with Beza about God?

3. What would you change of Beza's presentation of God if you were talking about God?

4. Why do you think it matters for Christians to think about God, deeply?

3

HOLY SCRIPTURE

IT IS CLEAR THAT if humans are to know God, it must be God who reveals who God is and what God does. The limits of human beings themselves along with the Christian conviction that humans are sinners and are cut off from a relationship with God means God must be revealed, in some manner, if humans are to know there is a God and what the nature and character of God may be.

Christian theology has spoken of God's revelation coming in two forms. There is Natural Revelation which is usually considered to be how God may be revealed through nature or the natural order. Some have argued that the existence of God can be established by the power of human reason. The medieval Roman Catholic theologian, Thomas Aquinas (1225–1274) famously posited "five ways" of proving God's existence.[1] This can yield a "natural theology." It is a "natural revelation" in that the power of reason can establish, by various means, that a "God" exists. Each of Aquinas' five "theistic proofs" ends with the phrase: "this is

1. See Aquinas's *Summa Theologiae*, 1a 2.3c.

what everyone calls God." While some have argued that everyone has access to this knowledge or "revelation" through reason, others have claimed God's existence can be known only from the perspective of faith.

The second form of God's revelation, spoken of by Christian theologians is God's "Special Revelation." God has been revealed at specific times and place and to particular people: in the events of the history of Israel and, for Christians, God has been revealed fully in the person of Jesus Christ. For Christians, the holy Scriptures of the Old and New Testament are the record of God's word and action and is God's special revelation. This conviction is received by faith—by God's revealing its reality to persons—by the work of God's Holy Spirit.

NATURAL/GENERAL REVELATION

In the early Reformed theological tradition, theologians and some Confessions of Faith recognized a revelation of God in nature. The French Confession (1559) said: "God reveals himself to men; firstly, in his works, in their creation as well as in their preservation and control" (Article 2).[2] The Belgic Confession (1561) spoke of God's being known, "first, by the creation, preservation, and government of the universe (Ps 19:2; Eph 4:6); which is before our eyes as a most elegant book, wherein all creatures, great and small, are as so many characters leading us to contemplate *the invisible things of God*, namely, *his eternal power and Godhead*, as the Apostle

2. Cochrane, *Reformed Confessions*, 144. Cochrane, in the tradition of the twentieth-century Reformed theologian Karl Barth, rejected the validity of a revelation of God in nature or natural theology. Cochrane wrote, that "the virus of natural theology" gained "admission in the French Confession," 139. He saw it then "spreading" to the Belgic Confession (1561) and the Westminster Confession (1647).

Paul saith (Rom 1:20). All which things are sufficient to convince men, and leave them without excuse."[3]

Both the French and the Belgic Confessions go on right away to say that God is revealed: "Secondly, and more clearly in his Word, which was in the beginning revealed through oracles, and which was afterward committed to writing in the books which we call the Holy Scriptures" (French Confession) and "secondly, he makes himself more clearly and fully known to us by his holy and divine Word; that is to say, as far as is necessary for us to know in this life, to his glory and our salvation" (Belgic Confession).[4]

Theodore Beza was concerned to establish the certainty of Christian belief. Through his career, as he engaged in polemics with Roman Catholics and other Protestants, Beza wanted Christian believers to be certain in their faith. His writings sought to help establish Christians in this way—so they knew what they believed and could give a reason for their faith. So Beza wanted to fortify what can be called "the objective aspect of belief."[5]

In this regard, Beza could look positively on a natural or general revelation of God in nature for what it entailed. He wrote: "When we behold the stars, when we consider the magnificence and magnitude of heaven, when we contemplate God in his works, it necessarily comes to mind: 'This was not able to happen by chance.'"[6] Beza continued in this

3. Cochrane, *Reformed Confessions*, 189–90. On Beza and the Belgic Confession, see Gootjes, *Belgic Confessions*.

4. Cochrane, *Reformed Confessions*, 144; 190 on the "twofold knowledge of God" (Lat. *duplex cognition Dei*). These confessions show what Calvin showed in the structure of his *Institutes* (1559): The Knowledge of God the Creator (Book I) and The Knowledge of God the Redeemer (Book II). See Muller, *Dictionary of Latin and Greek*, 97.

5. Mallinson, *Faith, Reason, and Revelation*, 96.

6. Mallinson, *Faith, Reason, and Revelation*, 100. From Beza, *Romains et aux Hébreux*, 30.

passage by indicating that nature provides some knowledge of God in God's various attributes such as God's wisdom, rule, goodness, power, righteousness, and perfection.[7] Humans have, for Beza, an intuitive and general knowledge of God. This is related to Calvin's emphasis of a universal "sense of divinity" (Lat. *sensus divinitatis*) and a "seed of religion" implanted in all persons.[8] Beza wrote:

> It is altogether true that a general notion that a Deity exists has been left in the mind of man, the knowledge of which is *confirmed and maintained* by a consideration of the Deity's creation above, around, and below. Even onto the smallest things he has engraved, as if with gigantic letters, his eternity and his existence as the Creator above all creatures. He shows his omnipotence, without which the world would neither have been created nor governed, his omniscience, which shows forth in the arrangement and direction of so many diverse creatures, and his absolute goodness, willing that there should be no mistakes at all. For he could create nothing but by his pure goodness.[9]

But natural or general revelation is limited. For Beza, as also with the Reformed Confessions cited above, "The Knowledge of God in Creation" does not have the power to bring salvation from the effects of sin or establish humans with the true and genuine knowledge of God which is found in "The Knowledge of God the Redeemer"—in God's special revelation: Jesus Christ. While natural revelation

---

7. Mallinson, *Faith, Reason, and Revelation*, 100.

8. Calvin, *Institutes*, 1.3.1 and 1.4.1.

9. Mallinson, *Faith, Reason, and Revelation*, 102. This is Mallinson's translation from Beza's, *Sermons sur l'histoire*. Mallinson lists the page number as 46. However, the correct page numbers are 53–54. The 1598, second edition, provides the quote on page 46.

can be seen as an expression of the general grace of God to humanity, it does not convey the fullness of God that is found in God's special revelation in Scripture. Natural revelation thus cannot stand on the same level as the Word of God in Scripture.

The power of reason has its limits, too. As Beza wrote:

> It is necessary for him to be vehemently distressed and confounded who struggles to comprehend the wisdom of God by his own finite reason. Answer this for me: if you should want to contain the ocean in a drinking cask, what else could you do but fail, and be rightly called insane? Yet even more tolerable, although inexpressible, is the proportion between the ocean and the smallest cup, than between the wisdom of God, and the foolishness of man's very corrupt mind.[10]

Mallinson commented: "For Beza, the highest insanity is for man to inquire into the mysteries of God by his a priori reason."[11]

The theological reason for this inability of human reason to know the mysteries of God is that by the Fall into sin, all humans (through Adam—Gen 3) the human faculties of reason and will have been corrupted so they cannot perceive or desire divine things (see ch. 6 below). Humans are not able to seek God (corrupt will) or know God (through reason). Beza said that "original sin" in humans have made persons "altogether inexcusable" before God (Rom 1:20). Humans have nothing within themselves which is not "altogether subject to and enthralled to this corruption." Though

10. Mallinson, *Faith, Reason, and Revelation*, 110–11, from Beza, *Tractationum Theologicarum*, 1:695. Cf. Beza, *Book of Christian Questions and Answers*, 70.

11. Mallinson, *Faith, Reason, and Revelation*, 111.

original sin has not "abolished in us the substance of the soul or of the body (farther than that thereby the body is made subject to corruption to return to dust and powder for a time), yet it has changed the light of the understanding into darkness, the integrity and uprightness thereof into all wicked qualities, and to speak in a word, has blotted out the image of God, which shone before in the first creation of man."[12]

Special Revelation: The Bible as The Word of God

The Scriptures are God's "special revelation." Uniquely, the Bible is the source of authority which does what natural or general revelation cannot do in itself. The Scriptures are the record of God's word and actions which instruct us for salvation—found in Jesus Christ, who is God's unique revelation. God speaks through the Scriptures in a unique and authoritative way, leading to the recognition that the Bible is the Word of God.

Beza, along with other sixteenth-century Protestant reformers, stressed the necessity and deep importance of holy Scripture. The Bible was the written word of God and source, the touchstone, and criterion by which Christian doctrine—and all Christian belief and practice is based.

Beza constantly worked with the Scriptures. As the book in which the living voice of God was heard, Beza was concerned to establish the best texts of the biblical books so the Scriptures could be read, interpreted, and applied to the lives of Christian believers. His work with the Bible had theological and pastoral dimensions. This work had wide-ranging influences. As one scholar noted: "In addition to sermons and commentaries on Job, Ecclesiastes and the Song of Songs (not to mention his lectures on Romans and

12. Beza, *Master Bezaes Sermons*, 109 (*Canticles*, 1.8.11).

Hebrews), Beza made crucial contributions to establishing the Greek text from which Protestant Bibles in the vernacular were to be produced."[13] Through it all, for Beza, "the point of exegetical [interpretive] work is to make it possible for believers to hear the truth of the Word of God."[14]

Beza began his *Book of Christian Questions and Answers* by asking:

> Who has set us in this world?
>
> Answer. God, of his own singular goodness.
>
> Quest. To what end?
>
> Ans. To the end that we should serve him: and that he should be glorified by giving eternal life to us.[15]
>
> Quest. What is the way to worship God aright, and consequently to attain eternal life, and to glorify him duly?
>
> Ans. To know and acknowledge him (Rom 1:21. John 17:3) after the same manner that God has disclosed himself to us in his word.
>
> Quest. What do you call the word of God?
>
> Ans. That which the Prophets and (God's word Eph 2:20) Apostles have received by God's spirit and committed to writing: which book we call by the name of the Old and New Testament.
>
> Quest. Who then is the author of those books?

---

13. See Farthing's entry in McKim, *Dictionary of Major Biblical Interpreters*, 193. An important resource is Backus, *Reformed Roots*. Backus shows that "Beza's 1598 N.T. had a crucial influence on AV 1611" [King James Version] and "his influence seemed to increase as Revision progressed," xix.

14. McKim, *Dictionary of Major Biblical Interpreters*, 195.

15. Beza, *Questions and Answers*, 1.

Ans. God himself. And the writers or (Rom 10:8; 2 Tim 3:16; 2 Pet 1:20) penners thereof were the Prophets and Apostles.[16]

Quest. How do you know that? (Acts 2:11; 1 Cor 1:17–24; Luke 21:15; Acts 6:10; John 5:30; Acts 17:11; 2 Cor 4:3)

Ans. The things themselves that are treated of those in writings: the majesty of God shining forth in that homeliness of speech; the heavenly pureness and singular holiness that utters itself everywhere in them; the most sure steadfastness of the principles whereupon that doctrine is grounded: and the laying together of the fore-sayings and of their fallings out: do enough and more than enough show these writings to be altogether divine and heavenly, and that the same is the most perfect doctrine of truth, though all the world should say never so much to the contrary. To the confirmation hereof makes also the orderly success of things done, and the record of godly men delivered from hand to hand. And (John 6:45; Acts 13:48; Phil 1:29; Acts 6:14) that I know these things in such ways, as I fully agree to matters which men are inclined partly to despise and laugh to scorn, and partly so to embrace, as yet notwithstanding they wrote not at all what they believe: I impute it wholly to the holy Ghost, who has opened my heart that I might both hear and understand these secrets (2 Tim 3:17).

---

16. Beza asked in his *Little Catechism* where God has set forth and declared how God wants us to know and serve God. His answer was: "In that book which we call the Bible, comprehending together with different histories, the Law and the Gospel." To the question: "Who has made this book?" Beza's answer was: "God himself, by the ministry of his holy Prophets and Apostles." Beza, *Little Catechisme*, A1.

Quest. Is all that we must believe for salvation, comprehended in those writings?

Ans. Altogether.[17]

From these questions and answers, it is clear Beza regarded the Bible as the word of God. Holy Scripture is where God has been revealed so God may be worshiped rightly. In Scripture, the gift of eternal life is revealed, and the ways God may be glorified are set forth. God's word is expressed by the prophets and the apostles. They had God's Spirit and committed to writing the Old and New Testament. It is "God himself," wrote Beza who is the "author" of Scripture. The "writers" or "penners" of Scripture were the human servants of God, the prophets and the apostles. This view is substantiated in Scripture itself as Beza cited Rom 10:8; 2 Tim 3:16; and 2 Pet 1:20. The "marks" or content matter of Scripture—including God's majesty and holiness shining through as well as its doctrines and prophecies "show these writings to be altogether divine and heavenly, and that the same is the most perfect doctrine of truth." The message of Scripture became meaningful, Beza testified because "the holy Ghost, who has opened my heart that I might both hear and understand these secrets (2 Tim 3:17)."[18] The full-

17. Beza, *Christian Questions and Answers*, 1–2.

18. On the question of the relationship between the "marks" of Scripture (internal and external) which Beza says show "these writings to be altogether divine and heavenly" and the "work of the Holy Ghost" who opens hearts to receive Scripture as God's word, Mallinson's view is that Beza's formulations "suggest that the Spirit simultaneously accompanies the objective evidence when dealing with the elect, and enables the mind to appreciate that evidence" (Mallinson, *Faith Reason, and Revelation*, 187). See his ch. 6: "The Authentication of Scripture." This issue relates to other scholarly questions about the relation of Beza's theological method compared to John Calvin's. Differing views are found among Beza interpreters, especially on the issues of the nature of Scripture and predestination. See the extended

ness of Scripture's revelation of the salvation God gives in Jesus Christ is fully conveyed in the writings of holy Scripture. To the question: "Is all that we must believe for salvation, comprehended in those writings?" Beza's answer was short and definitive: "Altogether"!

In his more technical writings, Beza expanded on descriptions of Scripture. In the *Propositions and principles of diuinitie propounded and disputed in the vniuersitie of Geneua, by certaine students of diuinitie there, vnder M. Theod. Beza, and M. Anthonie Faius* (1595),[19] the University of Geneva theological disputations, supervised by Beza and Faius, Beza recounted that the biblical books are those in which God has declared "both what he will have us to know concerning God, and what is to be done by us." The prophets and apostles who recorded Scripture were "inspired by God's Spirit."[20] The "whole Scripture" has been "given by the inspiration of God and is also called the word of God."

In the "providence of God," the canonical Scriptures have been "brought into a certain order and Canon—to distinguish them from 'counterfeit' writings. This applies especially to the books of the Apocrypha, which the Roman Catholic Church accepted."[21] The Scriptures are to be "a rule of faith and obedience"[22]

The canon of Scripture is recognized as God's word, said Beza, "not so much by the common consent of the Church, as by the testimony of the Spirit of God who

---

discussion in Wright, *Our Sovereign Refuge*, ch. 2: "Beza's Interpreters." Cf. Manetsch, *Calvin's Company of Pastors*, 241–45; and Rogers and McKim, *Authority and Interpretation*, 160–65.

19. Beza, *Propositions and Principles*, 231ff.

20. Beza, *Propositions and Principles*, 232.

21. Beza, *Propositions and Principles*, 233. Beza called these opponents "Tridentine conspirators,"

22. Beza, *Propositions and Principles*, 232.

teaches us, that they are to be embraced, as being most undoubtedly true, and that they have proceeded from God's own mouth."[23] This conviction was shared by all the sixteenth-century Protestant reformers: It is the work of the Holy Spirit that brings conviction that the Scriptures are the word of God.

The Scriptures "wholly contain all those things that are needful for our salvation." No additions to the Scripture are needed. "For the Scripture (as Paul expressly teaches) is able" to make God's people "absolute." It is a "most grievous" error when persons believe that "the saving knowledge of God is to be sought elsewhere than in the written word."[24] Beza was clear that Scripture itself is the "sole and true touchstone for proving true doctrine."[25]

Interpreting Scripture

Scripture, as the word of God, must be interpreted. For Beza, again following other Protestant reformers, "the natural and proper interpretation of holy Scripture is to be drawn from the analogy of faith, and the conferring of places." This principle (Lat. *Analogia fidei*) means that "individual doctrines are to be understood in light of the whole understanding of Christian faith, that obscure passages

23. Beza, *Propositions and Principles*, 233.

24. Beza, *Propositions and Principles*, 233.

25. Cited in Mallinson, *Faith, Reason, and Revelation*, 147, from the *Correspondance de Théodore de Bèze*, 3:262. The "touchstone" image for Scripture as constituted by the "Prophets and the Apostles" was used by Beza in his *Sermons Upon the Three Chapters of the Canticles*, 85 and 158. Cf. Manetsch, *Calvin's Company of Pastors*, who quotes Beza in relation to his own Confession of Faith: "I desire that each person who reads [my *Confession*] will compare it carefully with the Scripture, which is the sole and true touchstone for proving true doctrine" (228n35, citing Beza, *Confession de la foy chrestienne*, 5, 10).

of Scripture are to be understood in light of clearer portions, and the OT [Old Testament] in light of the NT [New Testament]."[26] Beza went on to indicate this means "that which is dark-like in one place, is in another clearly taught, that which here is shortly, is elsewhere largely set down"—thus the more "obscure" places are to be interpreted in light of the "clearer" places and those things mentioned briefly ("shortly") are more thoroughly explained in other places of Scripture.[27] In this sense, as other Reformers also said, Scripture is "self-interpreting." The different passages and texts of Scripture help interpret each other.

Beza went on to indicate that

> some places of the Scripture remain even to this day, so obscure and hard to be interpreted, so the very best and most faithful interpreters have not agreed among themselves, on their proper meanings. But in these things, every person is to acknowledge his own ignorance, sluggishness, or some other fault. The Scripture is so plentiful, that one and the same place can admit to different interpretations, and yet all agreeable with the doctrine of faith.[28]

The church does not experience unanimity when it comes to interpreting the Scripture. But a spirit of humility is to prevail in biblical interpretation as individuals acknowledge their own limitations. The richness and depth of the Scriptures means that while differing interpretations of individual passages or texts will be found, there can still be agreement overall on the "doctrine of faith." To Beza this meant that disagreements "notwithstanding," it is "certain that the grounds and necessary heads of Christian religion

26. McKim, *Westminster Dictionary*, 11.

27. Beza, *Propositions and Principles*, 234.

28. Beza, *Propositions and Principles*, 234.

are so clearly set down by the Prophets and Apostles, as (the Spirit of God working in the Saints) they are manifestly perceived in the Church."[29] Beza rejected the views of those who "think the Scripture so obscure, as it needs to be made clear by some other light."[30] This "other light," invariably, said Beza, would be from "the pretended Catholick Church" or from "the Fathers, from the Synods, or from some long custom of time"—as though, "the Scripture had not been understood, before either the fathers, or the Synods were."[31] Beza had earlier written that "the expositions of ancient Doctors" are to "be received as undoubted" only insofar as they "agree with the truth."[32]

Beza continued with this theme when he concluded of the church fathers that with respect to doctrine, "all their sayings are without prejudice, to be diligently examined, according to the rule of God's written Word"—which is "what they themselves everywhere in their writings wish to be done."[33] This relates to "government and ceremonies of the church" of their times. What must be distinguished is what the writings of the apostles "command to be perpetually observed in the Church" from "the matters that are indifferent and were added since their time." Attention must also be given to "circumstances, which are always necessarily subject to change."[34]

29. Beza, *Propositions and Principles*, 234.

30. Beza, *Propositions and Principles*, 235.

31. Beza, *Propositions and Principles*, 235.

32. Beza, *Propositions and Principles*, 234.

33. Beza, *Propositions and Principles*, 248.

34. Beza, *Propositions and Principles*, 248.

The Living Voice of God

Scripture as the word of God has to be interpreted. Beza's work on the text of Scripture was to enable the Scriptures as the source for knowing Christian faith to be better understood. Through sermons, pastors and preachers enable Scripture's message to be known and received in faith by the work of the Holy Spirit. The Spirit enables hearers to understand Scripture and personally appropriate God's word to and for their lives. Through preaching and the study of Scripture, the Bible becomes the living voice of God to those in the church who are God's elect.

The Bible is central to the lives of Christian believers. Scripture is the authoritative word of God, the source for our knowing who God is and what God has done, especially in the gospel of Jesus Christ. In Scripture, we hear the living voice of God.

In the opening of his *A Little Catechism*, Beza asked:

> [Qu. 6] What is the Gospel?
>
> [A.] That heavenly doctrine which teaches us, what we must believe to our salvation through Jesus Christ only.
>
> [Qu. 7] Doth this word contain all that we must believe and do?
>
> [A.] Yes, without having any need to add or join anything thereto, or to take anything there from.[35]

These answers set the directions for what the Scriptures as a whole and specifically the gospel of Jesus Christ provides. The gospel in the Scriptures contains what we must believe for salvation; and what we must do to be living as disciples of Jesus Christ and as the people of God; as Beza would say:

35. Beza, *Little Catechism*, A1 (Questions 6 and 7).

as the elect in the church. It is through the Scriptures, by the power of the Holy Spirit, that we believe—and hear the living voice of God in the Scriptures. As Beza put it: "Neither do I say there is any other cause of believing for us than that which is set forth in the books of both Testaments."[36] This statement clearly shows the importance of God's Special Revelation in Scripture for Beza. Scripture is, as other Reformers put it: Sola Scriptura—the sole source of our true knowledge of God and God's gift of salvation. As Beza wrote: "He who knows God apart from the Word knows nothing for salvation."[37]

In one of Beza's *Household Prayers*, "To Crave of God the Light of His Word," Beza spoke of the living Word of God found in Scripture. He was thankful that God had "revealed thyself unto [humanity] in a lively voice, by thy eternal word" in

> Eden, Horeb, in the burning bush, and elsewhere, afterward by thy prophets insinuating thyself by thy spirit into their hearts and thoughts, to the end by their ministry to instruct thy people: and finally that thou hast also manifested thyself in greater light by thy own word made flesh for our redemption, and speaking unto us by his mouth: Yea which is more, that thou hast so far graced us, that this thy word of life hath been, and still remains among us, faithfully collected in the sacred registers of the holy scripture, so to be unto us, the image of thy glory, the Law of thy Kingdom, the ladder to Heaven, the gate to paradise, the trumpet of salvation: to be brief,

36. Beza, *Tractationem Theologicarum*, 1:503, in Mallinson, *Faith, Reason, and Revelation*, 143.

37. Beza, *Tractationem Theologicarum*, 1:651, in Mallinson, *Faith, Reason, and Revelation*, 143. Cf. Mallinson's ch. 5.

the treasury of piety, virtue, wisdom, consolation, and perfection.[38]

Throughout the Scriptures, God was revealed and spoke to the people of Israel. God spoke in the "Word made flesh" in Jesus Christ, "speaking to us by his mouth." This "word of life" remains among us, "faithfully collected" in the "holy scripture." Beza went on to pray: "I beseech thee therefore (my God) vouchsafe to direct and guide me in the understanding of this eternal truth, through the operation of thy spirit, (the true teacher of our souls)."[39] The Spirit of God helps us to understand God's eternal truth which is the "word of life" to us.

God the creator of all things has chosen to be revealed to human beings—sinful as they are. This revelation, in nature, does not deal with the human problem of sin and how humans can be united with God in a relationship of trust and love, as God provided before sin entered the world. God's revelation of God's own self came to the humans who wrote the Scriptures—"prophets and apostles," and who conveyed God's divine revelation through what became the Bible—the "Word of God." These Scriptures are interpreted to humans—through the assistance of God's Holy Spirit. The Scriptures present the means of salvation through the death and resurrection of Jesus Christ. By the work of the Holy Spirit, the Scriptures are the means by which humans can hear the living voice of God.

Faith is the gift of the Holy Spirit which enables us to believe in Jesus Christ as our Lord and Savior. Beza said that no person will "be recognized as a Christian before

38. Beza, *Household Prayers*, D2.

39. Beza, *Household Prayers*, D4. Beza warned of our "malady" of wanting to make our own "natural sense" the "critic and judge of the wisdom of God, which is made known in his holy Word." Beza, *Sermons sur l'Historie*, 271, in Wright, *Our Sovereign Refuge*, 257–58.

God, unless he believes inwardly and shows it clearly on the outside."[40] The Spirit brings faith in the Scriptures as God's Word through which God speaks to and guides believers by the Spirit. Indeed, wrote Beza: "The only will of God being testified to us by his holy word, is the only true and immutable support of the true faith, seeing that it is the only rule of all true reason."[41] Scripture's authority is established by God as the Scriptures support true faith. God's voice speaking through Scripture is the supreme authority in the lives of believers since Scripture is the final judge or "rule of all true reason." God's Spirit speaks in and through the Scriptures.

Beza urged Christians to look to Jesus Christ who should always be before our eyes. Through the Spirit in Scripture, we see Christ, who "has left us his lively portrait in his doctrine written by the Apostles, comprising whatever is necessary for us to know, either through his person, or touching all the counsel of God his Father concerning our salvation."[42]

QUESTIONS FOR DISCUSSION

1. Do you find Beza's distinctions between "Natural/ General Revelation" and "Special Revelation" to be persuasive?

2. Why was it important for Beza to indicate Scripture's "author" was God; but that God worked through the human biblical writers?

40. Beza, *Sermons sur l'Historie*, 257, as translated in Wright, *Our Sovereign Refuge*, 251.

41. Beza, *Sermons sur l'Historie*, 259, in Wright, *Our Sovereign Refuge*, 252.

42. Beza, *Master Bezaes Sermons*, 31.

3. What are implications of recognizing that persons come to the belief that Scripture is the Word of God by the work of the Holy Spirit, rather than by their power of reason alone?

4. What are examples of Beza's conviction that the "plain" portions of Scripture help to interpret the more "obscure" portions?

5. In what ways do you experience Scripture as being "the living voice of God"?

4

JESUS CHRIST

WHO IS JESUS CHRIST? How can Jesus be both God and man? What did Jesus do? How did he fulfill the multiple functions (offices) which Scripture and theological tradition assign to him? What can be said of him that communicates all of these ideas effectively? All of these questions are investigated in Beza's *Propositions and Principles of Divinity.*[1]

Beza's treatment of Jesus is systematically driven by the Second Article of the Apostles' Creed. In fact, the whole of the *Propositions* is an exposition of the Creed, the Commandments, and the Lord's Prayer; three of the most important and formative collections of material in the whole of Christian theology.

These materials (Creed, Commandments, Prayer) were expected to be known by memory by members of Reformed Churches (and Lutheran and Catholic Churches

---

1. Beza, *Propositions and Principles of Divinity.* The English translation used here was published in London in 1595 and is based on the Latin original. In the citations which follow the short title *Propositions* will be used along with the page number of the material.

too for that matter) in Beza's day and he would and could expect them to be instantly accessible to readers of his theological treatises. Today, they are lesser known. For that reason, and to allow readers to follow along with Beza's argumentation, they are reproduced here.

THE APOSTLES' CREED

> I believe in God, the Father almighty, creator of heaven and earth.
>
> I believe in Jesus Christ, his only Son, our Lord, who was conceived by the Holy Spirit and born of the virgin Mary. He suffered under Pontius Pilate, was crucified, died, and was buried; he descended to hell. The third day he rose again from the dead. He ascended to heaven and is seated at the right hand of God the Father almighty. From there he will come to judge the living and the dead.
>
> I believe in the Holy Spirit, the holy catholic church, the communion of saints, the forgiveness of sins, the resurrection of the body, and the life everlasting. Amen.

THE TEN COMMANDMENTS

- You shall have no other gods before Me.

- You shall not make idols.

- You shall not take the name of the LORD your God in vain.

- Remember the Sabbath day, to keep it holy.

- Honor your father and your mother.

- You shall not murder.

- You shall not commit adultery.

- You shall not steal.

- You shall not bear false witness against your neighbor.

- You shall not covet.

THE LORD'S PRAYER

> Our Father, which art in heaven, Hallowed be thy Name. Thy Kingdom come. Thy will be done in earth, as it is in heaven. Give us this day our daily bread. And forgive us our trespasses, as we forgive them that trespass against us. And lead us not into temptation, but deliver us from evil. For thine is the kingdom, The power, and the glory, For ever and ever. Amen.

The importance of these materials for Beza's theology cannot be overstated and thus, again, their inclusion here. In particular, as mentioned previously, and yet worth repeating, the second article of the Creed is the organizing principle of Beza's *Propositions*.

When Beza, and other theologians throughout the history of the Church to his day, thought about and wrote about Jesus they determined that one aspect of their considerations had to focus on the question of the humanity and divinity of Jesus. To be sure, the humanity of Jesus was self evident to them. He was born, he lived, he died. He met all the criteria of human being. But he was also frequently described as being divine. Of being God in the flesh. The incarnation and the resurrection along with his miracles were scriptural evidence of this and this evidence was taken seriously, and literally, by theologians including Beza. But how? How could Jesus be both man and God? This claim was not made regarding any person in the Bible, Old or

New Testaments, but Jesus. The Father wasn't human, and neither was the Spirit. But Jesus was. Was he, then, 50 percent man and 50 percent God? 75 percent and 25 percent? The answer at the end of all the debates was that Jesus was "fully God and fully man." Theologians call this the "hypostatic union" and it was "codified" in the Athanasian Creed.

The relevant portion of the Athanasian Creed (regarding the full divinity and humanity of Jesus) declares:[2]

> Now this is the true faith: That we believe and confess that our Lord Jesus Christ, God's Son, is both God and human, equally. He is God from the essence of the Father, begotten before time; and he is human from the essence of his mother, born in time; completely God, completely human, with a rational soul and human flesh; equal to the Father as regards divinity, less than the Father as regards humanity. Although he is God and human, yet Christ is not two, but one. He is one, however, not by his divinity being turned into flesh, but by God's taking humanity to himself. He is one, certainly not by the blending of his essence, but by the unity of his person. For just as one human is both rational soul and flesh, so too the one Christ is both God and human. He suffered for our salvation; he descended to hell; he arose from the dead; he ascended to heaven; he is seated at the Father's right hand; from there he will come to judge the living and the dead. At his coming all people will arise bodily and give an accounting of their own deeds. Those who have done good will enter eternal life, and those who have done evil will enter eternal fire. This is the catholic faith: one cannot be saved without believing it firmly and faithfully.

2. "Athanasian Creed," https://www.crcna.org/welcome/beliefs/creeds /athanasian-creed.

Beza affirmed the Creed and explained this aspect of its teaching in his *Propositions*.[3] It is to Beza's exposition, then, of the doctrine of Christ as enunciated in that work that we now turn our attention. It is the fullest and most systematic of Beza's treatment of the subject and, accordingly, worth a careful look.

Beza begins with the most important question the Church asked about Jesus: how can he be both God and Man, divine and human, unborn and yet born, spirit and flesh?

THE TWO NATURES OF CHRIST

When believers think about the two natures of Christ they are first of all called upon to remember that this doctrine is critical to the faith itself. No Christian may rightly dismiss the doctrine nor may it be ignored. It should be understood. As difficult as this may be, it is required.

What, then, should believers know? First, that the union of the divine and the human in Jesus is such that there is but one person, and not two. There is not a human Jesus for his sojourn on earth and a divine Jesus who pre-existed in heaven and who exists now in heaven. "In Christ, therefore, there is not two separate Christs: one in heaven and one on Earth. There is no Christ God and Christ Man."

The problems with this understanding are immediately apparent. Did Jesus have flesh in his preexistence then? If not, how can it be the case that he is both human and divine in eternity? Beza provides a potential solution:

> Now although these two natures are inseparable,
> they do in fact remain distinct, both in them-
> selves and in their essential properties. And in
> their actions. Accordingly, the divine nature is

3. Beza, *Propositions*, 76ff.

an attribute of the divine and the human nature
is an attribute of his humanity.

Does Beza solve the problem? Unfortunately he does not in spite of spending five pages attempting to do so. The doctrine of the two natures of Christ is just as "mysterious" as the doctrine of the Trinity. And just as the mystery of the Trinity is beyond the capacity of the human intellect to grasp, so is the doctrine of the two natures of Christ. Beza and other theologians simply should have recognized the mystery and left attempted rational explanations aside as they invariably result in more questions being raised than they actually answer.

THE OFFICES OF CHRIST

It was relatively common by the sixteenth century to discuss Jesus the Christ in connection with what theologians called the "tripartite offices of Christ." By this they meant that when he was on earth, incarnate, Jesus fulfilled three roles: as a prophet, a priest, and a king.[4]

Beza followed Calvin here as he did in so many aspects of his theology. And yet his take on the subject bears his own image. Here's what Beza asserts:

Because humans are sinful, and cannot escape their nature, God appointed a mediator to rescue them from the brutality of their sinful condition. This mediator is Jesus the Christ. This same Jesus was represented in the Old Testament by the figures of the prophets, the priests, and the kings, and as such he fulfills their offices in his own. As a prophet he teaches people the will and the purpose of God. But as prophet he also brings to fruition all of the prophecies in the Old Testament which relate to him.

4. Calvin, *Institutes*, 2.15.

Jesus also embodies the kingdom of God and brings it into existence. He is, thus, a king. Indeed, he is the King of kings, the Lord of lords. In his kingdom all of his enemies are subjected to him and defeated by him, and that includes sin and death and of course the devil. But this is no earthly kingdom. It is a spiritual one.

And the priesthood of Jesus is comprised of both his act of sacrifice and himself as the sacrifice he offered. The priest makes himself the offering and this offering, being the sinless Son of God, is perfectly acceptable to God. It is, in fact, the only perfect sacrifice ever given to God.

Jesus, then, is the Prophet who fulfills all prophecy, the King who rules all kings, and the Priest who sacrifices the one and only perfect offering to satisfy both the judgment and the mercy of God.

While making these points Beza makes a few remarks to the side about the Jews and the papists and he describes the papists as worse than the Jews because they should know better than to reject Christ and yet they do regularly with their "sacrifice of the Mass" and other "ungodly" traditions.[5] At this point it is justifiable to remind ourselves that the sixteenth century had a huge anti-Semitic problem. Regrettably, many of the most articulate Reformers fell victim to the same terrible attitudes toward the Jews that history has seen in other times and places. This is no credit to them and it is, and remains, a stain on their reputations both as Christians and as theologians.

For example, Beza writes:

> The Jews are worthily condemned, along with all others who think that the Kingdom of God consists of outward pomp and ceremony; and even more impudent than the Jews are the members of the Roman Curia which imagines

5. Beza, *Propositions*, 81.

itself to be the very visible manifestation of the Kingdom of God![6]

It is a genuine pity that Beza and so many of his contemporaries were unable to see past the prejudices of their own day.

THE VIRGINAL CONCEPTION OF CHRIST

Like the majority of Christians before the Enlightenment and the rise of biblical criticism, Beza believed that Jesus was born by means of the virginal conception of Jesus. It is proper to describe the event as the virginal conception rather than the "virgin birth" because "virgin" (classically) describes a person who has not had sexual intercourse. And intercourse precedes birth (before of course the rise of artificial insemination). Jesus, according to the Creed, was born of the virgin Mary and that claim asserts that Mary was a virgin when Jesus was conceived and remained such till after his birth. Though, to be sure, the Catholic Church maintains that Mary remained a virgin her whole life while Protestants and Reformed generally holds that Jesus had half brothers and sisters (cf. Mark 6).

The notion of the virginal conception of Jesus has, however, in recent centuries, fallen on hard times. Nonetheless, Beza affirmed the doctrine, taking it quite literally. He observes:

> By conception we understand that that which was formed within the Virgin was true God and true man. And that the forming of the man in the womb was simultaneous to the uniting of the Word with the flesh of the man.[7]

6. Beza, *Propositions*, 81.
7. Beza, *Propositions*, 157–58.

Beza explains, furthermore, that the uniting of this divine Word with human flesh will continue for eternity. The divine nature of Jesus did not eclipse the human nature of Jesus, nor vice versa. The divine is preserved in the human and the human is preserved in the divine.

The overlap between the doctrine of the virginal conception of Jesus with the doctrine of the Two Natures of Jesus is both expected and sensible. Understanding the one requires understanding the other, which is why Beza frames them both in such similar ways. Jesus is exalted above the angels, but still fully human. Beza attempts to summarize this idea with a pithy little saying:

> Christ was rightly said by the Father to be great-
> er than himself, and lesser than himself.

Beza offers no scriptural proof for this claim however. He goes on to assert that while it is true that Scripture declares Mary to have been overshadowed by the Holy Spirit, it is not proper to describe the Spirit as the Father of Jesus. The Father sends his Son; the Son assumes human flesh; and the Spirit forms that flesh by the substance provided by the body of Mary.

And while Mary was sinful herself, she did not pass this sinfulness to Jesus because the Spirit cleansed the materials Mary's body provided which was the flesh of Jesus. Beza concludes his discussion of the virginal conception by denouncing various heresies which attempted to rebut the truth of the fully human and fully divine nature of Jesus.

THE BIRTH OF JESUS

The next portion of the *Propositions and Principles* addresses the topics of the birth, circumcision, and baptism of Jesus. Beza's views on these matters are fairly "conservative" in the sense that he conserves here the tradition of the Catholic Church that Mary is the Mother of God "though not the mother of deity."[8] Beza goes on to assert that the birth of Jesus is instructive for two particular reasons. First

> we learn that the Word, having taken upon himself our flesh, our soul, and our mind, that in all things (except sin) he might be like his brethren, commenced being God and man.[9]

The birth of Jesus unites the human and the divine. This simple apparent truism is critical for the doctrines of salvation and sanctification and it should not be surprising that Beza would make the point. It is essential that he does and he is well aware of that. What is surprising is that modern theology seems less interested in the birth of Jesus, which few see as miraculous in the first place. Albert Mohler observes (in an essay published by Baptist Press listing a number of theologians and scholars who reject the notion of the miraculous nature of the birth of Jesus):

> In America, the public denial of the virgin birth can be traced to the emergence of Protestant liberalism in the early 20th century. In his famous sermon, "Shall the Fundamentalists Win?" Harry Emerson Fosdick—an unabashed liberal—aimed his attention at "the vexed and mooted question of the virgin birth."[10]

Mohler would agree with Beza's first point regarding the importance of the Birth of Jesus, and many would not. Beza's second reason:

8. Beza, *Propositions*, 162.

9. Beza, *Propositions*, 162.

10. Mohler, "Virgin Birth," para. 4.

> The second, that by this means we might be assured that Christ, according to the flesh, is from Mary's ancestors, that is, Adam, Abraham, and David. These were those to whom the promise that a Messiah would come from their seed was made.[11]

Furthermore, he was also born according to the words of the prophets and thus fulfills all of their predictions concerning the coming of the Messiah. He was born in such a way, then, that he is the Messianic Mediator between God and man.

But did Mary remain a virgin after the birth of Jesus? Yes, Beza asserts, though he admits that Scripture itself is silent on the matter. So, he continues, this is not something to argue about or speculate about since Scripture's silence on the matter makes dogmatic assertions both unwise and ill-advised.

Beza discusses the childhood of Christ briefly, describing it as being normal and typical of children of the era. He cried. He breastfed, and grew as a normal child because "God would not have the laws of nature broken in those things." Beza also makes the interesting point that the circumcision of Christ demonstrates that he had a normal body as well. But so do the bits of Scripture where Jesus is described as hungering, thirsting, and being weary. He was a real human being. And all points attempted to prove the contrary made by the heretics were ruled out by Scripture itself.[12] Beza summarizes regarding the birth, and thus of the humanity, the human-ness, the creatureliness of Christ thusly:

11. Beza, *Propositions*, 163.
12. Beza, *Propositions*, 163–64.

> This Nativity was the beginning of the open humiliation of Christ whereby he made himself of no reputation and took on himself the form of a servant; thereby truly coming into the world even as his death and burial were part and parcel of that same humanity.[13]

The importance of the humanity of Jesus for Beza's theology cannot and should not be underestimated. Jesus genuinely was human. His birth, his circumcision, his baptism, his need to consume food, his need for drink, his need for sleep, his need of clothing, and the fact that he grew physically and spiritually and emotionally all point to this one central and critical truth: Jesus was truly man. That truth becomes key in Beza's exposition of the meaning of the death of Jesus, to which we now turn.

THE SACRIFICIAL DEATH OF CHRIST

The Apostles' Creed reminds us that "he suffered under Pontius Pilate, was crucified, died, and was buried; he descended to hell. The third day he rose again from the dead. He ascended to heaven and is seated at the right hand of God the Father almighty." These sentences are the core of the Christian faith. Jesus suffered, died, and rose from the grave. These are the elements of Christian faith that set it off from its parent Judaism and which continue to distinguish it from the other two great monotheistic religions of modern times: Jesus died and rose from the dead. Judaism doesn't hold to such a notion of Jesus, and neither does Islam. Both of which view Jesus as a great teacher but not risen from death.

Beza heartily, full-throatedly, embraced these core truths. He insists that Jesus, as soon as he assumed flesh,

13. Beza, *Propositions*, 164.

began the work of salvation.[14] This happened by virtue of the fact that Jesus was sinless and as the sinless Son of God he was both willing and able to fulfill the perfect will of God and display absolute obedience to the Law of God according to its true intentions if not according to the traditions of men (namely, the Pharisees).

Jesus, however, did not simply fulfill the will of God. He took upon himself our failures to do so. What humanity failed in, Jesus succeeded doing.

Jesus's suffering, as reported by the evangelists, was all part of the means by which sinners were reconciled to God. Beza focuses on these particular aspects of the passion of Christ: that he was the object of "the fearful hatred of God against every transgression of the Law which could only be appeased by a perfect satisfaction." And, Beza continues, "the unspeakable love of God toward humanity because he sent his only begotten Son so that whoever believes in him might not perish but instead have everlasting life."

God's hatred of sin, for which Jesus suffered, and God's love of humanity are the key factors in the sacrificial death of Christ. Beza embraced, then, the substitutionary atonement model of redemption. Jesus's death was by rights the death of every person. So that Jesus's life should be the life of every person who fled to him for refuge and redemption. The rest, tragically, being left to suffer for their own sins everlastingly.

Beza then insists that this plan of God was achieved by God's using Satan, the priests, Judas, and Pontius Pilate. God led them such that their own hatred of Jesus resulted in the very thing which God had intended to achieve—the redemption of the elect. Yet

14. For this and what follows in this section, see Beza, *Propositions*, 166–71.

as for the instruments, who did not sin because they were compelled to or against their own consciences, God allotted to them the just judgement their sins deserved.

God used these people's wicked intentions to result in the redemption of the chosen. Hence the death of Jesus, because of his perfect obedience, and his death on the cross, clothes the elect with perfect righteousness as the law requires because Jesus fully satisfied the will of God and provides sinners with the only path for the remission of sins.

Furthermore, Beza asserts:

> Christ, by his death, has abolished both the first and second death for his Elect. The first death, not fully destroyed (since the Elect continue to die physically), but that he has changed it in such a way that it is no longer a punishment for sin or an entrance into the Second (the everlasting) death but is instead their entry into everlasting life.

But what happened when Jesus died? Were the soul and body separated? Were the humanity and divinity severed? Beza insists that though Jesus body and soul were sundered at death, as is the case with every person who dies, Jesus continued to be both God and man. And as the God Man, Jesus descended into hell.

THE DESCENT INTO HELL

Where did the Reformers, and Christians in general, and Beza in particular, get the idea that Jesus descended into hell? None of the Gospels make any such assertion. Paul doesn't in any of his letters. There's nothing of it in Hebrews or James or even the book of Revelation. Jude doesn't speak of it nor does John in any of his three epistles. Second Peter also makes no mention of it. It is, in fact, only drawn from an obscure and uncertain few lines in 1 Peter (the relevant parts are italicized):

> For Christ also suffered once for sins, the just for the unjust, that He might bring us to God, being put to death in the flesh but made alive by the Spirit, by whom also *He went and preached to the spirits in prison, who formerly were disobedient,* when once the Divine longsuffering waited in the days of Noah, while the ark was being prepared, in which a few, that is, eight souls, were saved through water. (1 Pet 3:18–20 NKJV)

And, combined with this line:

> For this reason the gospel was *preached also to those who are dead,* that they might be judged according to men in the flesh, but live according to God in the spirit. (1 Pet 4:6 NKJV)

This rather mysterious line was then attached to Eph 4:9 (a Deutero-Pauline text, i.e., a text not written by Paul himself but by one of his disciples at a time shortly after Paul's own death):

> Therefore He says: "When He ascended on high, He led captivity captive, And gave gifts to men." (Now this, "He ascended"—what does it mean but that He also first *descended into the lower parts of the earth*? He who descended is also the One who ascended far above all the heavens, that He might fill all things.) (Eph 4:8–10 NKJV)

Thus armed, early Christian theologians began to assume and to teach that Jesus spent his time between his death and his resurrection in hell preaching to the inhabitants of that unhappy place.

Beza disagreed, instead believing that the Creed's mention of a "descent into hell" was merely metaphorical. The Creed's line

> was a summary of the last and lowest degrees of Christ's humiliation as a way of talking about all of the aspects of his suffering, crucifixion, death, and burial; a metaphorical way of describing his anguish and dejection so that "he suffered, died, was buried, and descended into hell" is just one article of the faith.[15]

Jesus didn't literally descend into hell. He did so metaphorically, in suffering. Beza makes use of just one scriptural proof for his case that the descent of Jesus into hell was metaphorical:

> And Jesus said to him, "Assuredly, I say to you, today you will be with Me in Paradise." (Luke 23:43 NKJV)

Jesus's words to the thief on the cross that he would, that very day, be with Jesus in paradise is all the evidence Beza needs to reject the literal meaning of the Creed's declaration that Jesus descended into hell and instead adopt a metaphorical reading. Further, if it had been truly a literal descent into hell, "The Evangelists would not have omitted such a thing."

His lengthy argument regarding the misunderstanding of the Creed ending, Beza insists:

> We simply understand, by the "descent into hell," those things which Christ being made a curse for us suffered in his soul for our sakes in those torments especially such that nothing more horrible can be imagined.[16]

15. Beza, *Propositions*, 175.

16. Beza, *Propositions*, 177.

Jesus suffered, died, and was buried. And then he rose from the grave.

THE RESURRECTION OF JESUS

Jesus overcame death. His body did not decay even in the slightest in the three days of his entombment. And his "full victory manifested itself in the resurrection of his body, because life is the opposite of death."[17]

Beza goes on to remark that it was only the body of Jesus which rose again, not his deity nor his soul because these things do not and cannot die. Yet the resurrection is the reuniting of the soul with the body, it's "proper instrument."

> The resurrection did abolish none of the essential quality of the body which has both a quality and a quantity, and to be finite. Hence it follows that it is also enclosed within the boundaries of its members, and is contained in a particular place.

The reason that Beza makes that particular point is because his next observation is that the notion of transubstantiation "falls to the ground," as does the notion of consubstantiation. Beza holds neither the Catholic nor the Lutheran views of the Supper to be legitimate. See the discussion of Beza's understanding elsewhere in this volume.

Jesus rose bodily. This is proven by the fact that after the resurrection he both ate and drank. And he rose bodily by the power of his own deity. Jesus raised himself from the grave. This demonstrates, according to Beza, that "his resurrection is a clear demonstration that he was truly God."

17. For this and what follows in this section, see Beza, *Propositions*, 198ff.

But why did Jesus wait three days to rise from the grave? Beza insists that this is because he did not wish to appear to have merely passed out or become unconscious somehow. And he did not wait longer so that the faith of the disciples would not be risked.

The key point, though, of the resurrection, was that it effected our salvation.

> The resurrection of Christ is the sure pillar of our resurrection, because the church is, as it were, the complement or filling up of Christ: and therefore taking away that chief doctrine of the Christian faith would end the preaching of the Gospel.

Our own resurrection thus guaranteed by the resurrection of Christ, Christians can feel confident in the fact that they will have, after death, "the very same body that lay down in the grave" will be raised.

Beza now makes an intriguing remark concerning the raising of the dead of the damned. The resurrection belongs to the elect and to the elect alone.

> The resurrection of Christ properly belongs only to the Elect. The wicked will rise again, not by virtue of his resurrection, but by the just judgment of God resulting in their eternal damnation because of the penalty for sin which was previously announced to Adam—"On the day that you eat it, you will die."

Jesus proved his resurrection by his numerous appearances, Beza asserts. But before he was raised his spirit was, in Beza's estimation, in paradise. Indeed it passed from his body into paradise and returned to his body at the resurrection. Consequently, when the elect die their spirits also pass from their bodies and arrive in paradise where they remain until the day of resurrection when they are reunited with their own bodies. These resurrected bodies are truly physical bodies, corporal entities, but of a far more excellent condition.

THE ASCENSION

Briefly stated, Beza is of the opinion that the ascension was as literally historical as the resurrection. And that Jesus's bodily ascension is evidence of his physical presence in but one location. He is not on earth. He is in heaven. Seated at the right had of the Father.

Yet Jesus is present on earth, in the church and the world, through the person of the Holy Spirit. He will return, bodily, to earth, at the restoration of all things. But he goes further, clarifying thusly:

> Yet we say that God and man did ascend, because his human body was taken up by along with his divine being, being inseparably joined to his human nature, and is presently there in a manner mysterious to us.[18]

Beza mentions the appearance of Jesus to Stephen and Paul as examples of the bodily ascension. After all, Stephen saw him standing at the right hand of God. But Beza also wishes to show that the ascension was a sort of "victory march" over his earthly foes. When he ascended, he marched past and over all of the powers he had defeated by his resurrection. This is the real "triumphal entry," not to an earthly Jerusalem but to the heavenly City of God.

Furthermore, the ascension demonstrates, as though further demonstrations were needed, the divinity of Jesus.

18. Beza, *Propositions*, 204 and following for this section.

It also shows that he has returned to the glory he knew before the incarnation.

And finally, Jesus ascended in order to prepare a place for the elect in the presence of God. "For where the head is, there the members must also be." We also will ascend to heaven to take up residence in the home which Jesus has himself prepared for us. He ascends to lead us home: "Hereby a way is opened for us to our heavenly country, from whence we fell by the sin of Adam."

Beza's understanding of the ascension of Jesus aligns perfectly with his theological program: to show clearly to his students and congregants and readers that the proper understanding of theology is both morally relevant and spiritually significant. Proper theology feeds the soul. Bad theology poisons the spirit. Beza will now examine the next phrase of the Creed: he was seated at the right hand of the Father. Or, in more theological terminology, Jesus was exalted.

THE EXALTATION OF JESUS

In the world of the Bible, the era of Israel, the divided monarchy, the exile, and the postexilic periods as well as into the so-called Second Temple Period it was customary for monarchs to have seated at their right hand their chief advisor. So when the New Testament talks about Jesus being seated at the right hand of God, "Now this is the main point of the things we are saying: We have such a High Priest, who is seated at the right hand of the throne of the Majesty in the heavens, a Minister of the sanctuary and of the true tabernacle which the Lord erected, and not man" (Heb 8:1–2 NKJV), it is referring to his position of power as second only to the Father alone.

Beza understands this and he also follows the line of thought laid out in ancient Israel and the New Testament: Jesus is God's "right-hand man." But Beza's reading of the situation is a bit more theologically nuanced. He sees the seating at God's right hand as a figurative description of the assuming of Jesus of the power of the Father such that the Father and the Son are perfectly and absolutely equal (with the Spirit as well).

His seating (or re-investiture in the heavenly court) shows, furthermore, that he

> most powerfully accomplished the office . . . and became Conqueror, Ruler, and triumphant and as such has obtained a perpetual governing over all creation, both to preserve and to bring to full salvation as well as the utter defeat of his enemies.[19]

The government of Christ being established, he rules the world and all that is in it in conjunction with the ruling power of the Father and the Spirit. But his rule is not perfected and will not be perfected until the last day. The day of judgment. Accordingly, what Christ is presently achieving is the empowering of his own children and the subduing of their enemies as well as interceding for his own to the Father. Finally, then, we turn our attention to the last portion of Beza's treatment of Jesus Christ: Jesus's return.

JESUS RETURN IN JUDGMENT

Jesus is coming again. The claim is made in the book of Acts when, at Jesus's ascension, the two men in white asked the disciples why they were still standing around when Jesus

19. Beza, *Propositions*, 208–9. The remainder of this section draws from those and the following pages.

had told them to remain in Jerusalem until the promise of the Spirit came, and at any rate, he would return again just as he had departed.

Paul also asserted the return of Jesus as did the book of Revelation. Thus it was natural that the Creed pick up the concept and that Christians from very early on as well asserted the belief. Beza, unsurprisingly, is no different.

Beza's exposition of the doctrine begins with an assertion that Jesus will return when the full number of the elect are gathered and the time established by the Father's plan arrived at. But Beza also cautions against any speculation concerning the how and when, writing:

> It is inappropriate and profane to speculate what
> form the final restitution of all things will take,
> beyond what the word of God reveals.[20]

When Christ does return, all humanity will stand before God in judgment. Those judged condemned will be sentenced to hell and the elect will enjoy the benefits of heaven. Beza provides biblical texts for these assertions.

> Christ will come from heaven in his physical,
> visible body clothed in his eternal divine glory
> and majesty, bearing his name which is above
> every name.

The remainder of Beza's exposition of the doctrine repeats the previously stated beliefs that Jesus will deliver the elect and that the godless will be condemned. He condemns those who would suggest otherwise, including Origen and those who followed him who insisted that even the devil would be saved at the end.

20. Beza, *Propositions*, 213ff., for this portion of the Creed's exposition.

Beza believed it when the church maintained the Return of Jesus Christ. And so he taught it, along with the other doctrines scantily mentioned in the Apostles' Creed, concerning Jesus.

QUESTIONS FOR DISCUSSION

1. Beza believed in the literal virginal conception of Jesus. Do you agree with his assertion?

2. Beza also believed in the literal bodily resurrection. What do you think of this belief?

3. Do you believe that it is necessary to believe as Beza did in order to be a faithful Christian?

4. Do you think Jesus is coming again? Why or why not?

5

HOLY SPIRIT

THE HOLY SPIRIT IS the Third Person of the divine Trinity. The Spirit shares fully in the life of the Trinity with God the Father and God the Son. Compactly, Beza wrote: "We believe in the Holy Ghost who is the coeternal and consubstantial power of the Father (Gen 1:2) and the Son, in whom he is resident and from whom [the Spirit] proceeds (John 14:16, 26) being one God with them (Rom. 8:9–11) and nevertheless distinct in person (Matt 28:19)" (4.1).[1]

This formulation expresses the consensus of the orthodox Christian theology developed in the early Christian centuries on the nature of the Holy Trinity.[2] The Holy Spirit's person is fully equal to the Father's and Son's while the Spirit shares a distinct personhood. The nature and work of the Holy Spirit is made clear in the holy Scripture's. References to the "Spirit of God" and the "Holy Spirit" indicate

1. References in this form are to chapter and section of Beza, *Briefe and Pithie Summe* (1565).

2. See chapter 1 above.

the specific works of the Spirit throughout the history of redemption.

Beza's discussion of the Holy Spirit in his *Brief and Pithy Sum* is the longest chapter in this book. Beza devoted fifty-one articles to this topic. His emphases throughout are not so much on the person of the Spirit as on the work of the Spirit, particularly in bringing faith to the elect for salvation. Beza indicates what faith is and how it is expressed. Throughout, Beza continues to be aware of the pastoral question of whether or not one has true faith in Jesus Christ. Beza also deals with the question of the role "good works" play in the Christian life. In conclusion, Beza discusses the work of the Spirit in the church in relation to the sacraments of Baptism and the Lord's Supper.

The Person of the Holy Spirit

In his description of the Holy Spirit (4.1) Beza was aligned with the western church's interpretation of the Nicene Creed with the Spirit "proceeding from the Father and the Son." The Spirit "proceeds" and is fully equal in power and glory with two other members of the Godhead as "one God." Thus "the name of God, is some times personally attributed to him." The implication of this is that "the holy Ghost is therefore to be worshipped, by the one and the same faith and invocation, that the Father and Son are."[3]

Like the Scriptures themselves, Beza's primary interest in *A Briefe and Pithie* is conveying the work of the Spirit in relation to the church and salvation. He wrote he will consider the Spirit: "according to the effects which He brings forth in the children of God, in beginning with His grace (Rom 8:12–17), to make them feel the efficacy and virtue thereof; and briefly to bring them from degree to degree to

3. Beza and La Faye, *Propositions and Principles*, 4.3.

the right end and mark to which they are predestined before the foundation of the world (Eph 1:3–4)" (4.2). The Spirit's work has effects as the Spirit is the agent or means or person of the Godhead who establishes God's grace in a person's life and leads them into understanding the meaning and power (efficacy) of their election to salvation through faith in Jesus Christ.

The Holy Spirit and Salvation

Central to the work of the Holy Spirit is the establishment of faith in the elect of God. The Holy Spirit makes us "capable and fit to receive (Eph 1:17) the same Jesus Christ, which He does in creating within us by His mere divine goodness and mercy what we call faith, the only instrument of taking hold of Jesus Christ (John 3:1–13, 33–36) when He is offered to us, and the only vessel to receive Him" (4.3). The Holy Spirit creates faith in the elect since faith is the divine means by which salvation is received. Faith is focused on Jesus Christ. Those in sin can "take hold of Christ" by faith which is enabled by the work of the Spirit. Only through faith can Christ be received. The "ordinary means" the Holy Spirit uses to bring faith is through the preaching of the word of God and the sacraments celebrated in the church (Matt 28:19–20; Acts 6:4; Rom 10:17; Jas 1:18; 1 Pet 1:23–25) (4.4).

Due to our "natural corruption" and the pervasive power of sin in humanity, we are "but dumb (Ps 51:15), deaf (Ps 40:6), and naturally blind (John 1:5)." This means "it is impossible for us to believe of ourselves (John 12:38–39) as it is impossible for a man that is dead to fly" (4.5).

But the God who has elected us has declared that God has so loved the world that God gave God's only Son, Jesus Christ (John 3:16), so that all who embrace Christ by faith will not perish. The faith we need is given by the Holy Spirit of God. This faith is "not to believe only that God is God and that the contents of His Word are true (for the devils have this faith and cannot but tremble at it, James 2:19), but we call faith a certain knowledge (1 Cor 2:6–8) which the Holy Ghost by His grace alone and goodness engraves more and more in the hearts of the elect of God, by which each one of them being assured in his heart of his election, applies and appropriates to himself the promise of his salvation in Jesus Christ" (4.5).

Seeing faith this way, connects Beza with John Calvin who wrote that "we shall possess a right definition of faith if we call it a firm and certain knowledge of God's benevolence toward us, founded upon the truth of the freely given promise in Christ, both revealed to our minds and sealed upon our hearts through the Holy Spirit."[4] Faith is not only an intellectual knowledge—such as believing Scripture is the word of God. But Beza and Calvin indicate faith is a "certain knowledge," given by the Holy Spirit to the hearts of believers in which salvation in Jesus Christ is personally applied and appropriated. This is a deep and certain knowledge, giving the assurance of salvation.

Since this assurance is grounded in the work of the Holy Spirit, it can be received and trusted. Beza continued: "Faith, I say, believes not only that Jesus Christ is dead and risen for sinners (Rom 8:16, 39), but proceeds to embrace Jesus Christ in whom only she trusts and so assures herself of her salvation that she doubts not (Eph 3:12)." Beza amplified this point with an apt citation from the theologian, Bernard of Clairvaux (1090–1153) who said that according to Scripture: "If you believe that your sins may not be put away, but by him whom you have offended, and also who is not subject to sin, you do well. But yet join to that another

4. Calvin, *Institutes*, 3.2.7.

point, that is to say that you believe also that by him your sins be forgiven. And this is the witness which the holy Ghost brings in our hearts, saying: 'Your sins are forgiven you.'"[5] The internal witness of the Holy Spirit is a personal witness in which the promises of the Christian gospel are made real and personally appropriated by those who are given the gift of faith whose object is Jesus Christ. Jesus Christ is "the mark of our faith" (4.6). For Beza, this meant that "all that is necessary for our salvation" is in Jesus Christ and "one that has Jesus Christ by faith has all" (4.6). For "in having Jesus Christ by faith, we have all things in Him (Rom 5:1); as the apostle says 'there is no condemnation to those who are in Jesus Christ'" (Rom 8:1).

Theologically, Beza said St. Paul affirms justification by faith alone. Faith is the means or instrument God uses to give the gift of salvation in Jesus Christ. For

> faith is the instrument which receives Jesus Christ and as a consequence receives His righteousness, i.e., all perfection. When we say then as St. Paul said that we are justified by faith alone (Rom 5:1; Gal 2:16–21; Phil 3:9; 2 Tim 1:9; Titus 3:5; Heb 11:7), it is not to say that faith is a virtue which makes us righteous in ourselves before God (for that would be to set ourselves in the place of Jesus Christ, who alone is our perfect and entire righteousness); but we understand that we are justified by faith because it embraces Him who justifies us, i.e., Jesus Christ, in such a way that it unites and knits us together with Him to be partakers of all the goodness which He has—which being granted and imputed to us, is fully sufficient to make us perfect and accepted for righteous before God (4.7).

5. 5.5; from Bernard's "First Sermon on the Annunciation."

Faith is the means of our union with Jesus Christ and the way by which those who believe in Christ receive of "all the goodness" Christ has. Christ's goodness or righteousness is imputed to us and makes us "perfect and accepted for righteous before God." Salvation by faith does not bring "arrogance or presumption" (Rom 8:16, 38; Heb 10:22–25) but instead takes all pride from ourselves and gives glory to God (4.8). In faith, we are taught to "go out of our own selves" and "know that in us there is nothing but the matter of damnation, and sends us to one alone—Jesus Christ, by whose justice [righteousness] alone it teaches and assures us that we will find salvation before God. For all what is in Jesus Christ (i.e., all righteousness and perfection) is counted and granted to us as properly our own, so that we embrace him by faith" (4.8).

This means that since "the just shall live by faith" (Rom 1:16–17; Gal 3:11), faith finds all that is necessary for salvation in Jesus Christ. For, said Beza, "we have now nothing else of our own, but Jesus Christ, and all that he has (John 17:9–11, 20–26), provided always that we be by faith united and conjoined with him as partakers of all his goodness" (4.9).

This is why, wrote Beza, that the church—the "assembly of the faithful is called the spouse of Jesus Christ her husband (Rom 7:2–6). This is to show the conjunction and communion which is between Jesus Christ and those who are joined with him by faith. For by virtue of this conjunction and spiritual marriage by faith, he takes all our miseries upon himself, and we do receive all his treasures from him by his pure goodness and mercy" (4.9).

The Holy Spirit and the Christian Life

Those who are justified by faith and joined with Jesus Christ in the "assembly of the faithful," the church, need a true and abiding faith, a faith that can withstand the assaults of Satan, meant to sow doubt and despair.

Beza considers several of these temptations that assail the saints (4.10–13). In them all, the Christian's recourse is not found within one's self. We must always turn to Jesus Christ and his righteousness as our salvation and as the way that one can withstand the onslaughts of the tempter's power.

1) God's infinite perfection and our infinite sinfulness (4.10) should lead only to eternal death (Rom 6:23). God's righteousness must be satisfied; the merits of the saints bring us nothing and have "no place to profit us."

To answer Satan, Beza writes that one should say to Satan:

> You will say then that there is infinite iniquities in me which deserves eternal death. I do grant it, but I add more to it which you have hastily, maliciously omitted, i.e., the iniquities which are in me were most sufficiently avenged and punished in Jesus Christ who has borne the judgment of God in my stead (Rom 3:25). So upon this I make my conclusion contrary to yours, i.e., for inasmuch as God is righteous and will not be paid double, and Jesus Christ, God and human (2 Cor 5:19), has by one infinite obedience made satisfaction to the infinite majesty of God (Rom 8:33). So it follows that my iniquities can no more distress or trouble me (Col 2:14), my accounts and debts being assuredly razed and wiped out by the precious blood of Jesus Christ, who was made accursed for me (Gal 3:13), dying as righteous for the unrighteous (1 Peter 3:18).

2) Satan may also assail by claiming we do not have the righteousness God requires of us. God requires humans should fulfill the whole law of God—meaning loving God perfectly and loving one's neighbor as oneself. Bring forth this righteousness or how will you bear the curse of the law and face the majesty of God (Deut 17:6; Gal 3:10–12) (4.11)?

To answer, Beza wrote:

> For here is declared a perfect obedience according to the Law, which was never found but in Jesus Christ alone. Let us learn here again to appropriate to us by faith another treasure and benefit of Jesus Christ, that is, His righteousness. For we know that it is He that has fulfilled all righteousness (Matt 3:15; Phil 2:8; Isa 53:11), having perfectly obeyed God His Father and perfectly loved His enemies (Rom 5:6–10), so that He became accursed for this, as St. Paul says (Gal 3:13), i.e., He bore the judgment of the wrath of God for them (Col 1:22; 2 Cor 5:21) so that we being clad with His perfect righteousness which is imputed to us by faith (as though it were properly our own) must be made acceptable before God as brethren (Eph 1:7–8) and co-heirs with Jesus Christ (John 1:12).

3) Satan may attack us by appealing to the natural corruption and original sin that affects all persons? Though you are clothed in the righteousness of Christ, "you are corrupted by nature, in which always remains the root of every sin (Rom 7:17–18). Now, do you, enemy to all uncleanness (Job 4:17; Ps 1:6), dare to appear before the majesty of God, who sees the bottom of your heart (Ps 44:21)?" (4.12).

To answer, Beza indicates: "Since the sanctification of Jesus Christ is imputed to us as our own, then the natural corruption (Rom 8:1–3) which rests partly yet in us cannot come into account, since it is covered and clothed with the holiness of Jesus Christ, who is much more able to sanctify and cleanse us before God than the natural corruption is to defile and corrupt us."

In all temptations and assaults on Christians, an underlying question is whether or not we have a true faith? Beza had written that it is not enough only to believe that "Jesus Christ came to save sinners, but that every one of us must particularly apply to himself and appropriate Jesus Christ to himself in such a way that he concludes within himself, 'I am in Jesus Christ by faith and, therefore, I cannot perish, but am sure of my salvation' (Rom 8:1, 38–39; 1 Cor 2:16; 1 John 5:19–20)" (4.13).

Does this personal appropriation of faith in Jesus Christ happen to us? Beza said: "We must examine ourselves as to whether we have this faith or not."

To this, Beza urges that one "ascend by the effects to the knowledge of the cause which works them" (4.13). When one has genuine faith in Jesus Christ, two effects will result, said Beza: The first is the testimony the Holy that we are children of God and leads us to cry "Abba Father" (Rom 8:15–16; Gal 4:6). The second is the genuine change made in our lives. This is what Scripture calls "regeneration" and "sanctification" (John 3:3; Eph 4:21–24). These are seen as workings of the Holy Spirit to make us a "new creation" (2 Cor 5:17), passing "from death to life" (John 5:24; Rom 6:13).

These actions of the Spirit bring three effects: "For as natural corruption holds our persons captive both in body and soul, working in us both sin and death, so likewise the power of Jesus Christ comes and takes possession of us and brings to us three effects: mortification of this corruption, which the Scriptures call the 'old man'; the burying thereof; and finally the rising and restoring of the new man, as St.

Paul describes these things (Romans 6 and throughout this epistle; 1 Peter 4)," wrote Beza (4.13). The Holy Spirit initiates and is intimately involved in the changes in persons' lives in which they becomes a "new creation." They now are led with new purposes and directions in living out the will of God in Jesus Christ.

These three effects are actions of the Spirit but they are all the result of "the work of Jesus Christ," as Beza indicates. The Spirit's work is to apply the work of Christ in the lives of those who receive the gift of faith. The Spirit always witnesses to Christ—and does not focus on the Spirit's own self. The Spirit points to—and applies—the work of Christ, particularly Christ's death on the cross which is the means by which sin is forgiven and new life becomes a reality!

Thus Beza argued that when these effects happen by the work of the Holy Spirit: to bring death to the "old man," the burying of the old life, and the rising and renewing of the new person—when these are realities and "if we feel them working in us, the conclusion is infallible—that we have faith and consequently Jesus Christ in us unto eternal life (as we have said). Thus it appears that all believers ought chiefly to have respect and to hold fast this precious jewel, which is the testimony of the Spirit of God which He gives to His elect by continual invocation and prayer to him, and to make them develop by continually exercising good works according to their calling [vocation] and the gift of regeneration which they have received (Rom 12:9–16)" (4.13).

To know this regeneration or new life certainly, Beza said, "we must come to the fruits of it." A person who is made "free from sin" and one's "natural corruption by the virtue of Jesus Christ dwelling" within "begins to do those things which we call good works." "The truth is," said Beza "that this faith of which we speak can no more be without good works than the shining sun without light or fire without heat" (1 John 2:9–10; Jas 2:14–17).

It is thus slanderous for opponents to say Beza and his colleagues in faith disapprove of good works or reject their importance (4.14). Beza spent five articles of his Confession of Faith discussing good works (4.15–19). Important here is Beza's emphasis that Scriptures teaches there are two great works God requires of Christian believers: Prayer and Love of Neighbor. These are prompted by the Holy Spirit.

Prayer. "Among all the fruits that faith brings forth universally in all Christians, we think that calling [invocation] on the name of God through Jesus Christ is the chief. We call this prayer. It is most acceptable to God whether we ask anything of Him or render thanks to Him" (4.16).

Prayer proceeds from a spirit of trust that God will hear and answer prayers. We ask God and do not doubt (Jas 1:6–8; cf. Matt 21:22; Heb 4:16; Mark 11:24; Heb 10:22). Prayers are made to our intercessor and advocate, Jesus Christ, who is "the only Mediator between God and man." Christ is our "perpetual advocate" (John 14:12–14; 16:23; 1 Tim 2:5; 1 John 2:1; Heb 7:25; 9:24) and as our intercessor: "Whom will we find that loves us so well as He that gave His life for us; yes, even when we were His enemies" (John 15:13; Rom 5:8)?

We must always remember that "our requests are not grounded on any worthiness that is in us, but only upon the excellence and dignity of Jesus Christ alone (who is promised and communicated to us by faith with all His benefits)." Our prayers proceed in the confidence that "we are assured that as much as we are reconciled to God by the Son (who is our only sufficient intercessor and advocate), we cannot fail to obtain those things which we desire that are expedient for us through Him. And without this confidence, it is impossible to be heard." Faithful confidence in God's willingness to answer our prayers is grounded in God's reconciling act in Jesus Christ, who intercedes and advocates for those who pray.

This led Beza to conclude that "following then the rule of Holy Scripture and the authority of the good ancient fathers, we esteem and allow true prayers to be the most agreeable things that Christians may offer to God among those commandments of the first table. Therein is contained an express confession of the goodness of God as well as his power, with the fear and reverence due to Him alone (Matt 6)." Praying is central for Christian life. God's goodness and God's power make prayer the Christian's heartbeat!

Works of Charity. Along with prayer, the Spirit prompts Christian believers in the church to carry out works of charity or love to others. Wrote Beza: "We esteem works of charity toward our neighbors which proceed from true love of God according to the commandment of the second table [of the Law, the Ten Commandments]. For we are reconciled to Him in Jesus Christ for whose sake we love our neighbors, although they may hate us. For otherwise, all that we do is worth nothing, whatever show or appearance it has in our life, as Jesus Christ declares to us by the example of the Pharisees" (4.16).

The work of reconciliation of sinners with God in Jesus Christ, by the work of the Holy Spirit, leads to works of love offered to neighbors. Faith in Jesus Christ is expressed practically and meaningfully in love shared for all—even those who may hate us. Without love, there is nothing of importance or value (see 1 Cor 13). On the broader, social scale, the care for the poor in Geneva and the work of deacons, as a church office, are expressions of this love impulse grounded in God's redemptive action in Jesus Christ.

In Geneva, the "organizational structure for charity" was the *Bourse français.* The Genevan church, as did other Protestants, "emphasized charity as a response of love to God and one's neighbor."[6] The *Bourse français* was the "fundamental institution that cared for not only many humble refugees and the poor of Geneva but also for French refugees."[7] Deacons in the church were charged with distributing the money collected for the care of the poor and sick.[8] As a leading pastor, Beza was involved with the *Bourse française*. Rights to the proceeds from the translation in verse of the Psalms by Beza were to be given to the *Bourse française*.[9] Beza gave exhortations to "be charitable"[10] and he continued the work of Calvin who sought funds from various cities for special collections for times of religious crisis.[11]

Good Works. Other works, says Beza, are "neither good nor evil, but only having respect to that end as they may serve to dispose us or support us in those works which are good." These enable Christians to be more ready to serve God; and these works are pleasing to God insofar as they follow from faith.

Beza is clear that any "good works" Christians do have their origins not in the will of fallen and feeble sinners. They emerge only through God's Spirit expressing the will of God, who has elected, called, and drawn believers

6. Olson, *Calvin and Social Welfare*, 12.

7. Olson, *Calvin and Social Warfare*, 11.

8. McKee, *John Calvin on the Diaconate*, 110. McKee points out that Rom 12:8 was the verse that is "the most distinctively Reformed of the various biblical texts concerned with the diaconate," 185. The Latin Vulgate term *tribuit* in this verse was translated in Beza, *New Testament* as *distribuit*, 187.

9. Olson, *Calvin and Social Welfare*, 54.

10. Olson, *Calvin and Social Warfare*, 250n85.

11. See McKee, *John Calvin on the Diaconate*, who indicates Calvin's first campaign for this purpose was in 1545 with Beza's campaigns being in 1567–1569 and 1572 (109–10).

together. Since humans do not possess a "free will" which enables them to do anything good in the sight of God, "grace must make us good trees before we can bear good fruit, it follows that there is no meeting together of grace and free will. For the Spirit of God has by His pure grace made us free from sin in uniting us by faith to Jesus Christ, from whom we get a new life to bring forth fruit to God" (4.17). Good works "come from Jesus Christ dwelling in us, by whose power and virtue we do them by grace, as the corrupt nature of Adam in which we were born brings forth sin in us" (4.18).

Clearly, as Beza maintains, "faith goes before good works." For "we must of necessity be justified and so consequently have just title to salvation before we can do any good work. In this lies all our consolation—that we have our only refuge in the special grace and mercy which is presented to us in Jesus Christ alone, who is not our Savior and Redeemer in part, but altogether" (4.18).

Good works are not the means to salvation; they do not save us or grant eternal salvation. We are saved only by faith in Jesus Christ. But good works are the necessary expressions of faith. If "faith without works is dead" (Jas 2:26), then the good works of Christians are ways of expressing basic faith in Jesus Christ as Lord and Savior.

Beza listed several benefits of good works in the Christian life. First, good works serve our neighbors. They also "provoke unbelievers to give glory to God" (Matt 5:16; 1 Pet 2:12; 4.19).

Second, good works "assure us more and more of our salvation, not as causes thereof, but as testimonies and effects of the cause—which is of our faith" (4.19). Good works are witnesses and demonstrations of our faith in Jesus Christ.

Third, no one's "good works" merit God's favor in themselves. But the good news is that believers can confess "the goodness of our God to be so great" that God considers us as God's children, not in ourselves, but "in Jesus Christ, his well-beloved Son," with whom we are "united and joined by faith." God looks at our good works, not as coming from us by our own powers or wills—but as works done in Jesus Christ, with whom we are joined by faith. God sees our works in Christ. Further, God also regards the "fruits" of God's graces, not as being "polluted by our infirmities and weaknesses." God accepts them because "they have proceeded or issued" from God. God accepts and allows our good works, blessing them in our lives (Gen 15:1; Matt 5:12; 10:42; 2 John 8) and giving spiritual blessings (1 Tim 4:8; Matt 19:29; 25:21).

Fourth, "good works are certain testimonies of our faith and also assure us of our eternal election. For faith is necessarily joined to election" (4.19). For "faith is no other thing than an assurance we have that the promises of eternal life pertain to us, because we were predestined and elected to it." While some may consider the doctrine of election to be a "curious and incomprehensible thing, it is to the contrary." For when tempted (by Satan) to doubt our election, Beza said we should not first seek "resolution in the eternal counsel of God whose majesty we cannot comprehend." On the contrary: "We must begin at the sanctification we feel in ourselves to ascend up more highly, since our sanctification (from whence good works proceed) is a certain effect of faith (Rom 8:5–9); or rather of Jesus Christ dwelling in us by faith."

The result of proceeding in this way is to realize that "whoever is united to Jesus Christ is necessarily called and elected by God to salvation." This means they will "never be rejected or forsaken" (John 6:37). So, said Beza, "it appears that sanctification with the fruits thereof is the first step or degree by which we begin to ascend up to the first and true cause of our salvation, i.e., of our free, eternal election. For whoever says that he believes and notwithstanding does not govern his life by the Spirit of God declares that he is a liar and deceives himself (1 John 2:3–6). For this reason, St. Peter admonishes us 'to make our calling and election sure' by good works (2 Peter 1:10)." To summarize: Good works are not "the cause or foundation of our calling and election, for St. Paul declares plainly the contrary (Rom 4:2)." But "since good works are a certain testimony to our conscience that Jesus Christ dwells in us, consequently we cannot perish having been elected to salvation (1 Peter 3:21; John 6:39)."

Beza's detailed discussion of the place of good works in the Christian life is undergirded by his doctrine of the Holy Spirit's work in the lives of Christian believers. The Spirit is active in guiding believers in doing good works, which are testimonies to one's faith in Jesus Christ, and of one's eternal election by God.

QUESTIONS FOR DISCUSSION

1. In what ways are you aware of the Holy Spirit as a person—and not just a "power" or "force"?

2. Why is it important to recognize it is the work of the Holy Spirit who brings faith and the gift of salvation in Jesus Christ?

3. What are ways you receive assurance of salvation by recognizing salvation comes by the work of God's Holy Spirit?

4. What are ways you are aware of the Holy Spirit's help in helping you face temptations toward evil?

6

SIN AND SALVATION

THE STORY OF SIN and salvation was central to Beza's theology. This story speaks of God and humanity. It describes the sin that has separated humanity from its Creator; and the actions of God to bring salvation to those whom God has elected or predestined to receive the gift of salvation through Jesus Christ.

SIN

Theodore Beza took sin seriously. He did so because sin is treated this way in holy Scripture. Basic to understanding sin is the understanding of who God is. Beza wrote that "God is perfectly righteous (Ex 20:5; 2 Cor 6:14). It follows that He neither will, nor may suffer any injustice to go unpunished. He is also perfectly merciful (Ex 34:6). It follows that the good which He does to man, He does of His full and sole grace" (3.3).[1] God, who is just and merciful, both

1. References in this form are to chapter and section of Beza, *Briefe and Pithie Summe* (1565).

judges injustice while also providing mercy. God's good actions in justice and mercy emerge from God's full grace; and solely by God's grace.

God, said Beza, has "not only foreseen but also eternally ordained to create humanity to spread forth and declare God's glory (1 Cor 11:7) in saving by God's grace, those whom it pleases him (Rom 9:23). God does not forget his justice, without which God cannot be God and God condemns others by his just judgment (Ex 9:16; Rom 9:22)" (3.6).[2] God's election is God's saving those to whom God chooses to give salvation while God carries out condemnation of others by divine, just judgment.

To carry out God's work, God created humans "good and pure." This was what must be expected, "God Himself being good"—therefore God "can do nothing but what is God." If humans had been created "wicked or evil," God would not be able to punish "the wickedness of which He Himself was the author and maker" (3.7). Thus God created humans as an expression of God's essential goodness—and in a blessed relationship with their creator. As Beza said: "The Lord then, at that time which seemed good to Him to execute His eternal counsel, created man male and female, after His own image and likeness (Gen 1:27; Eccl 7:29), that is, endued with righteousness and true holiness" (3.9). Humans created in the image of God were righteous and holy—thus reflecting the nature of God; and also being able to have a relationship with God—as the story of Adam and Eve in the book of Genesis, indicates.

---

2. Beza led into this statement by writing that "there shall be some saved and some damned, and all for the glory of God, as the whole Scripture declares." It follows that since "nothing happens or comes to pass at a venture or by chance" and that "God never changes his purpose or his mind."

But the humans created in the image of God chose not to live as they were created. Humans by their own willing choice and "without any compulsion" (Gen 2:17; Rom 5:12) joined themselves to the "devil, and therefore became culpable of the first and second death" along with all their "posterity." The results of this choice to disobey God and give in to the power of disobedience, represented by the "devil" plunged the whole human race into two deaths (3.10).

Original Sin

The first death means that human nature is corrupted in the descendants of Adam. This leads to "the separation of the soul from the body with the putrification of the body." All humans die (3.11).

The second death has eternal significance. Sin has meant "the inward corruption of the whole man, no part excepted (which we call original sin, Gen 6:5; Ps 51:5; John 3:6)," said Beza; and this makes every person, "even from the very first beginning of his conception, the child of wrath and subject to the second and eternal death" (3.12). This "corruption makes us altogether unprofitable." Humans stand "contrary to all goodness and wholly subject to sin." Citing Augustine, Beza continued to say that the human will, "vanquished by sin into which it fell," lost its "liberty" (Augustine, *De perfectione justitiae hominis*, 4.9). Humans use their "free will" in evil ways and have "lost it" and lost themselves (Augustine, *Enchiridion*, 30). While humans may labor and search to find whatever "good there is in their own will"—they "do not know how" to "find any" (Augustine, *De peccatorum meritis*, 2.18.28). This "original sin" resulting in humanity's sinful nature leads to a second death—an eternal separation from God (3.13).

FREE WILL

Humans are "without excuse" for their sin against God, said Beza (3.14). Humans still maintain their "natural faculties and powers." These have not been taken away because of sin. But they have been corrupted: "reason, judgment, will, and such others." This brings sinners into "darkness and enmity against God." Humans still have the "power to think, will, or do good or evil." But despite this kind of power or freedom to choose the sinful will "cannot nor will not (John 3:6; Rom 8:7) anything but altogether evil as long as the nature of man not being regenerated (that is to say, not healed and restored by grace) is not only wounded or hurt, but utterly and altogether corrupted and also willingly becomes the servant of sin." Humans cannot choose to will the good, which God desires. As Augustine said, wrote Beza: "The fault which follows the sin and which is its punishment has turned liberty into necessity [*De perfectione justitiae hominis*, 4.9)." Again, "free will as it is bound and in thrall [bondage], is worth nothing but to sin and fall [Augustine, *Ad Bonifacium*, 3 =*Contra duas epistolas pelegianorum libri*, 3.8.24]."

The effects of original sin are far-reaching; and deadly. Beza summarized these as "three kinds of sin":

> Original sin then is a full corruption of the whole nature of man. This corruption is transmitted from Adam into all his race and brings forth in humanity three kinds of sins. The first comprehends every inward motion and thought in man's understanding, although the will gives no consent to it. For God requires that God be loved with all the understanding and we have already said that it is utterly and altogether corrupted. The second kind of sin is when the will and affection consent to it. The third is when

humans even force themselves to execute what inwardly they have conceived and willed. (3.15)

The effects of human sin are the most serious and far-reaching consequences imaginable! Humans are cut off from God; and can do nothing by their own powers to change their situation—even if they "wanted" to do so. But sin means their wills are bound to evil ways; and not to the ways of God.

The only hope for humanity is for God to act to forgive sins and bring humans into the relationship which humans before the "fall into sin" could have with God. God's mercy and justice are both to be upheld. Beza wrote:

> So now there remains nothing but that all the world should run to ruin and destruction (Rom 3:19), but that God being not only most righteous, but also most merciful, had eternally ordained a means to cause all those things to turn to His great glory: to wit, to the greater declaration of His infinite goodness (Rom 3:21–25) towards those whom He has also ordained and chosen eternally to be glorified in their salvation (Rom 8:29); and likewise to the declaration of His power and wrath (Rom 9:22) by the just judgment and condemnation of the vessels of wrath prepared for destruction. For as St. Augustine said very well, if all were delivered, that due to sin by justice would be secret and hidden; what grace had given and granted would not be seen [Epistle 103 (=194), Ad Sixtus, 2.5]. (3.16)

God turns human sin to God's glory by being righteous and merciful. God eternally provides a means to declare God's "infinite goodness" to those God has "ordained and chosen eternally to be glorified in their salvation." Likewise, God's power and wrath are expressed in God's "just judgment and condemnation" of sinners. If all were "saved," God's justice would be "secret and hidden"—and God's grace would not be seen. God's grace is seen; and salvation is established by Jesus Christ, the only Mediator between God and humanity who through his death and resurrection provides the means of salvation for those God has elected to have faith in Jesus Christ as their Lord and Savior.

SALVATION

Beza focused on Jesus Christ as the One through whom salvation is given and received by those who believe in Christ as their Lord and Savior. He spoke of this in his *A Little Catechism*:

> [Question 1] Shall all the world be saved?
>
> [Answer] No, for the greater part of the world refuse their salvation.
>
> [Question 2] Who then are they which shall be saved?
>
> [Answer] They that have faith and believe.
>
> [Question 3] And what is faith?
>
> [Answer] A certain persuasion and assurance, which every true Christian man ought to have, that God the father loveth him, for Jesus Christ his Son's sake.
>
> [Question 4] Wherefore do you say for Jesus Christ's sake?
>
> [Answer] Because that we being altogether corrupted and wholly perverse in ourselves, God could not love us, but in respect of him only, which is man altogether just and perfect, that is to say, Jesus Christ his son.
>
> [Question 5] Does this faith come from ourselves?

[Answer] No, but from the only grace and goodness of God, who does freely give it to his elect and chosen ones.

[Question 6] And they who have this faith are they saved?

[Answer] Yes of necessity, for God hath given his Son to the end that everyone who believes in him, should have life everlasting: and he is not a liar.[3]

Here we find Beza's conviction about salvation and how it is accomplished and applied.

Beza begins by acknowledging that not all the world will be saved or receive salvation. In fact, not even the "greater part of the world receive their salvation." This is because salvation comes from having faith in Jesus Christ. This faith in Christ is "a certain persuasion and assurance . . ." Faith is not intellectual apprehension, a characteristic of knowledge or the understanding. Instead, faith is an inner persuasion and assurance of the truth that one is loved by God the Father and is loved for the sake of Jesus Christ.

It is through Jesus Christ that one is loved by God. In ourselves, humans are "corrupted and wholly perverse." This is the devastating power of sin. Sin corrupts human nature making humans "enemies" of God (Rom 5:10). Thus humans do not deserve to receive God's love. God loves a person through Jesus Christ—who is the One who is, himself, "just and perfect." For the sake of Jesus Christ, God's Son—God loves a sinner.

This faith in God's love in Christ does not come from one's self. Faith is not self-generated. Faith comes only from the "grace and goodness of God." Out of God's grace, undeserving sinners receive God's love. God's goodness is an

---

3. Beza, *Little Catechisme*, Fourth Section.

expression of who God is. God is one who in mercy, loves sinful persons. This is the grace given to God's "elect and chosen ones" by the Holy Spirit. Grace comes from God and is not "earned" in any way by sinners. Grace is God's free gift, given for salvation.

Are they who have this faith saved? Yes, said Beza: "Yes of necessity, for God hath given his Son to the end that everyone who believes in him, should have life everlasting: and he is not a liar." The purpose of God giving the Son, Jesus Christ is so that "everyone who believes in him may not perish but may have eternal life," to quote John 3:16. Those who, by faith, receive Jesus Christ, God's Son, as the expression of God's love, forgiveness of sins, and means of bringing salvation—are saved! God's promises are true—God is "not a liar," God is faithful (1 Cor 1:9) and salvation for sinners is found in Jesus Christ.

ELECTION AND PREDESTINATION

Faith is the gift of the Holy Spirit. The faith that brings salvation is the gift of God, given by God's Spirit to enable them to recognize and confess Jesus Christ as their Lord and Savior.

This theological conviction brings with it the question of to whom does the Holy Spirit give the gift of faith? Is salvation given to all persons? Can one desire the gift of faith and not receive it? These issues and others are related to the doctrines of predestination and election. These are historic Christian doctrines dealing with God's work of salvation.

Beza mentioned election and predestination in a number of his works. But in his most detailed theological treatment, *Tabula praedestinationis* (1555), also known as *Summa Totius Christianismi*,[4] his goal was to present a

4. This work was published in Beza's *Tractationes theologicae,*

positive statement about predestination in light of negative criticisms of Calvin's views from his opponents, especially Jerome Bolsec, who was banished from Geneva in 1551.[5] Beza prefaced this work with a chart which laid out in schematic form the elements of salvation and reprobation, as two streams coming from God.[6] Some have noted that Beza was not intending to provide a complete discussion of all Christian doctrines, or a *Summa theologiae*, like Thomas Aquinas (1225–1274) produced. Instead, the title of the book is better understood as "the sum total of the Christian life."[7] This is to be a discussion of Christian life, from and to all eternity. Beza's treatment includes "Aphorisms" which are biblical and theological discussions of the points on the chart. Thus, Beza's "fundamental intention," is

> to demonstrate how such a doctrine (as the order of the causes of salvation and damnation) belongs to Christian instruction and is a support

---

1:170–205. An English translation is the *Briefe declaration*, trans. William Whittingham. It was reprinted in 1575, 1576, 1581, and 1613. References to this English translation, here, are from the 1613 edition and paraphrased at points. This work is a primary work over which scholars have discussed the degree to which Beza represents a variance from Calvin's views and the growing "scholasticism" of Reformed theologians after Calvin. On this, see Wright, *Our Sovereign Refuge*, 55–71. Cf. Wright, *Theodore Beza*, ch. 5. Beza's later work *De Praedestinatio* was written in light of attacks on predestination as taught by Calvin by Jerome Bolsec (see *Tractactiones*, 3:402–47).

5. For further backgrounds and context, see Manetsch, *Calvin's Company of Pastors*, 135–136, and Trueman and Clarke, *Protestant Scholasticism*, 33–61. Calvin commended Beza's book in 1562. See Wright, *Theodore Beza*, 123.

6. John S. Bray commented that "the decree of predestination, itself, was based upon and derived from the nature of God." See Bray, *Beza's Doctrine of Predestination*, 72.

7. See Bray, *Beza's Doctrine of Predestination*, 72; cf. Trueman and Clarke, *Protestant Scholasticism*, 34.

of piety. In short, the intention of the *Tabula* is to show that the doctrine of the decree and its execution, as presented through the collation of biblical texts, is a source of consolation and strength—in this particular context, against the claims of Bolsec that the doctrine was not based on a simple reading of Scripture and was a monstrous distortion of the gospel.[8]

Structurally, the *Tabula* has eight chapters. The first chapter introduces the work, advocating for "the homiletical and pastoral use of the doctrine of predestination."[9] Chapters 2 through 6 present Beza's doctrinal teachings on the doctrine. Chapters seven and eight show predestination's use and application.

Chapter 1 is titled: "That the Question of God's Eternal Predestination is Neither a Matter of Curiosity Nor of Little Necessity in the Church of Christ." Beza appealed to Augustine (354–430) to say the church should learn that predestination is a proper subject to be discussed in accord with God's word in Scripture. Also, the doctrine should be handled so the church will be built up or edified. Beza was concerned with "the application of election to the life of piety."[10]

Christians should preach the doctrine to all, realizing that "only those who have ears to hear do hear us quietly, and to their comfort; and in those that have them not, this sentence is fulfilled, that hearing with their ears, they do not hear, for they hear with the outward sense, but not with the inward consent" (4–5). We do not ultimately know why

---

8. Muller, "Use and Abuse of a Document," 35. Wright wrote that "Beza applied the truth of predestination to his readers. He was a consummate pastor" (*Theodore Beza*, 126).

9. Muller, *Christ and the Decree*, 80.

10. Muller, *Christ and the Decree*, 80.

some "hear" and others do not. Only God knows. But the church is responsible to preach and obey God's commands. Augustine urges to "preach predestination, that those who have ears to hear may hear, and rejoice in God, not in themselves for the grace of God toward them" (7–8).

Chapter 2 is titled "Of the Eternall Counsel [Plan] of God Hid in Himself, but Which Afterwards, is Known by Its Effects." Here, Beza presents seven points (Aphorisms) which he believed were in continuity with the historic views of the church, represented by Augustine.

In the first Aphorism, Beza notes three things:

1) We cannot understand the ways of God and God's choices. They "cannot be found out" and are thus inscrutable. (9)

2) God has decreed all things that come to pass in creation, according to the "determinate and unchangeable purpose of God's will." (9)

3) God has decreed even evil—but God remains good since evil is carried out by "evil instruments" who carry out evil because they want to do so. (9–10)

In the second Aphorism, Beza indicates God has created two different ends for people:

Whereof God makes the one sort (which it pleased him to chose by his secret will and purpose) partakers of his glory through his mercy, and these we call according to the word of God, the vessels of honor, the elect, the children of promise, and predestined to salvation: and the others, whom likewise it pleased him to ordain to damnation (that he might show forth his wrath and power, to be glorified also in them) wee doe call the vessels of dishonor and wrath, the reprobate, and cast off from all good works. (10–11)

God's eternal choice is the highest source of determination, of all things.

In the third Aphorism, Beza indicates God's election of God's people to salvation is not determined by God's foreseeing that certain people will have faith; or from any "good works," anyone may attempt to do. God's election is "only of his own good will [good pleasure], from whence afterwards the election, the faith, and the good workes spring" (11). God alone is the author of salvation.

The fourth Aphorism mentions the issue of the assurance of salvation. Doubts may arise as to one's faith and calling or there may be times when Christians do not see "the fruits of faith" in their lives. In times like these: our only hope is God's eternal election in Jesus Christ. We know that in Christ, who is "our head," we are elected and only of his own good will, from whence afterward the election, the faith, and the good works spring forth, only of his own good will, from whence afterward the election the faith and the good works spring forth adopted—all by the will of God's eternal purpose (12). God's eternal purpose, made known in Jesus Christ is the solid ground of assurance.

The fifth Aphorism focuses on the reprobate, those decreed for destruction. This action of God—like election—is also inscrutable. "The first cause" of the damnation of the reprobate is only God's "just will, which we must with all reverence obey," since it comes from God, "who is only just and cannot by any means, nor by any person," in any way, be "comprehended" (13). The "whole fault" in reprobation "be in themselves"—in the reprobate. In contrast to election—in which the elect do not deserve their election; in reprobation, the reprobate deserve what they receive.

In the sixth Aphorism, the "purpose of reprobation" is acknowledged as hidden to us. But the causes of reprobation are clear: "corruption, lack of faith, and iniquity" within persons themselves (13–14). Humans are responsible for these causes, since they are "voluntary" (14).

In the seventh Aphorism, Beza indicates there is a distinction between the "purpose of election" (which God himself has decreed) and "election itself," which is "appointed in Christ."

Chapter 3, "God's Common Actions Toward the Elect and the Reprobate" (15), establishes God's justice in the damnation of the reprobate while also maintaining that God is gracious in electing a people to love and serve God.

Beza indicates God did not create persons sinful. If that had been so, then God would be the author of sin. Adam and Eve were created in the image of God. God is the author of good and not of evil. The first parents had a fully free will to choose obedience to God's will or to their own wills. But they proceeded to sin, even as this was by God's "will" or "decree." For "the whole fault of the reprobates' damnation lies within themselves," while on the other hand, "all the glory and praise of the elect's salvation belong wholly to God's mercy" (16). "Humans binding . . . the whole nature of man to sin, and so consequently to the death of body and soul" (17).

Chapter 4, "By what order God proceeded to declare and After a Sort to Execute His Election," features Beza's recounting of the history of salvation. Human sin was so pervasive and debilitating that humans could not save themselves. God's will and action was for the Father to send the Son into the world, as a divine and human person (God-man) to serve as a priest and die for God's elect. As Beza put it: "With one only offering and sacrifice of himself, [Jesus Christ] should sanctify all the elect: mortifying and burying sin in them, by the partaking of his death and burial: and quickening them into newness of life by his resurrection:

So that they should find more in him, then they had lost in Adam" (25).

God establishes a way to unite the elect to Christ. The Holy Spirit works to show and convict sinners of their sin. The Spirit draws them into union with Christ, by faith: "believe in Christ." The Holy Spirit's work is to regenerate the elect since persons cannot do that by their own power. God's grace enables true Christians to persevere in faith.

In chapter 5, "After what sort almighty God doth execute, and Effectually Declare his Counsel, touching Reprobation," Beza contrasted Christ who died for the elect with the reprobates who are sinners due to Adam: "For as Christ the second heavenly Adam, is the foundation, and very substance, and effect, of the elect's salvation: so also the first earthly Adam, because he fell, is the first author of the hate, and so consequently of the damnation of the reprobate" (35–36). All humanity is under either the "first Adam" or the "second Adam."

But those condemned are not condemned by Adam's sin alone. Humans themselves bear responsibility so that "the whole cause of their damnation, might be of themselves." Humans were "fallen willingly into that miserable estate" (36). God is thus just in condemning them because they are "corrupt" (37).

Beza went on to distinguish the steps that lead to reprobation. There are four different types of reprobates. The first of those are those whom God permits never to hear the gospel of Christ. They "walk in their own ways, and run head long to their perdition" (37).

The second type of reprobate is those who hear the gospel of Christ but can't and won't respond. They are not of the elect and "being called," they "hear not" (39). "When they are called to the feast, they refuse to come." Thus, "the word of life is folly to them, and an offense, and finally the savor of death to their destruction."

The third type of reprobate is those to whom God grants a general faith. But this faith will not bring salvation (39–40).

The fourth type of reprobate is "the most miserable of all" (40). They are "raised so high by some gift of grace, that they are a little moved with some taste of the heavenly gift: so that for the time they seem to have received the seed, and to be planted in the Church of God, and also show the way of salvation to others" (40). But "the spirit of adoption," which comes to those of God's elect does not appear in those who turn away from the gospel and that spirit of adoption is "never communicated to them." "For were they of the elect," wrote Beza, "they should remain still with the elect" (40–41). The condemnation of these is due to the Lord's decision and also to them, as sinners who follow their own ways. Their turning away from the gospel is "because of necessity, and yet willingly," since they are "under the slavery of sin" and "fall away from faith" (41). Their "corruption" leads to their just condemnation by God (42).[11]

Chapter 6, "Of the last and full execution and accomplishment of God's Eternal Counsel, as well towards the Elect as the Reprobate," provides a biblical and doctrinal conclusion to Beza's treatise.

Here, Beza wants to convey the ultimate end of the elect and of the reprobate. It is necessary, Beza wrote, that God "should save the just, and condemn the unjust" (43).

---

11. Beza wrote: "The execution then of the ordinance of election (that is to say, the salvation of the chosen) depends on faith that takes hold of Christ; and the execution of the ordinance of reprobation, that is to say the damnation of the castaways, depends on sin and the fruits thereof." Beza, *Book of Christian Questions*, 82.

Most basically: Those joined by faith to Christ are: grafted, rooted in him, and made one body with him. They are "justified and sanctified in him, and by him." So it follows that "the glory" which is their destination is "to the glory of God" and belongs to them "as by a certain right or title" (43).

On the other hand, those who "remain in Adam's pollution and death" are "justly hated by God" are condemned by God (43).

The end or purpose of God's judgments is "to set forth manifestly God's glory to all people" (46).

Chapters 7 and 8 focus on "How this Doctrine Should be Preached" and "Using the Truth of Predestination Personally."

Most important is that preachers avoid "vain and curious speculations" (50). The simple truth of Scripture is to be proclaimed in teaching about God's mysterious plan of predestination. Biblical language should be used to expound faithfully what the Scriptures teach (52). Preachers should maintain a balance in teaching about predestination—not going from one extreme to another or overlooking the means God uses in dealing with people. The minister's duty is to "lift up and comfort the afflicted consciences, with the testimonial of their election; and again, to wound and pierce the wicked and stubborn, with the fearful judgment of God" (56). In the end, final judgment belongs to God.

Beza's final chapter seeks to show Christians that when applied to their own lives, predestination should be a source of confidence and comfort instead of doubt. Only believing in God's eternal counsel or decree can produce certainty or assurance of salvation. God elects and God continues to give the gift of perseverance in faith (58). This assurance means "we might learn to assure and confirm our faith against all brunts [shocks; stresses] that might happen" (58–59).

Instead of speculating about God and God's counsels, one can begin with one's own life. Ask: Am I being sanctified? Do I have faith in Christ? If so, we have certainty—from these "effects"—that we have been called by God's voice in Jesus Christ. For the Scriptures witness that "all those that God has, according to his counsel, predestinated, to be adopted as his children through Jesus Christ, are also called in their time appointed—yes and so effectually, that they hear the voice of him who calls, and believe it so that being justified and sanctified in Jesus Christ, they are also glorified. Will you then, whatever you are, be assured of predestination" (62). In this, said Beza, one can be "assured . . . not by doubtful conjectures, or our own fantasies, but by arguments, and conclusions, no less true and certain than if you ascended into heaven and had heard form God's own mouth, God's eternal decree and purpose" (62–63).

QUESTIONS FOR DISCUSSION

1. In what ways do you see the effects of "original sin" being lived out in human lives?

2. Why does the seriousness of sin make God's provision of salvation in Jesus Christ such a work of God's great mercy and love?

3. What are your thoughts about Beza's treatments of election and predestination?

4. What do you find to be the comfort and joy of God's election and predestination?

7

CHURCH AND MINISTRY

Beza's understanding of the church was crucial to his entire theology. He saw the whole activity of salvation which God has provided by God's grace to be "in vain," if "there were not certain people who felt and tasted of the fruit and advantage of it"[1] This "certain people" is the church, the elect of God, those who have received salvation by the work of Jesus Christ on their behalf.

Christ's "eternal kingdom" has "subjects" whom God has chosen by grace from "the beginning of the world" to be a "congregation and assembly of people." These have "acknowledged and served the true God" according to God's will through faith in Jesus Christ. This church and assembly "shall last forever" and can withstand all assaults of "the devils in hell" can devise against them (78).

"Without Jesus Christ," there is no salvation, wrote Beza; and those who die without being a member of this "congregation and assembly, is excluded and locked out from Jesus Christ and his salvation." For salvation belongs

1. Beza, *Briefe and Pithie Summe,* 77.

only to those who acknowledge Jesus Christ as "their God and only savior."

NATURE OF THE CHURCH

Beza's further discussion of the church describes the nature of the church as related to God's salvation in Jesus Christ. There can be but "one true church." Since there is only "one God one faith and only one Mediator between God and man, even Jesus Christ" who is the "head of his church," there can be "but one church," Beza argues. This church is "catholic"—spread throughout the world. Since God has chosen people from "all nations" as has seemed "good" to God to do so, then the church is a "universal church."[2] The church's members are spread everywhere, "dispersed over all the earth."

This universal nature of the church means that since the church has one head, Jesus Christ, then all who are members of Christ by faith, wherever they may be, are joined together and "knit together" as "inhabitants of one community." This evokes the image from the Apostles' Creed in which the phrase "communion of saints" is used as a description of the relationship of those who have faith in Jesus Christ with each other. All, in the communion of saints, share in "the goods and treasures of Jesus Christ." Christ is their head and they are "members of him" since Christ unites and joins them to himself. Christ makes them alive ("quickens") them, justifies and sanctifies them. Christ, the head, unites who have faith in him with each other in the communion of saints.

Unlike the Roman Catholic tradition where the term "saint" is used for those who are especially holy or virtuous, Beza maintains—as do other Protestants—that in Scripture,

2. Beza, *Briefe and Pithie Summe*, 79.

"this word Saint is attributed to all faithful, living yet in this world, for as much as they have attained to Jesus Christ by faith, their only righteousness and sanctification."[3] All Christian believers share a common faith in Jesus Christ as their Lord and Savior. They are united with Christ by faith; and they are united with each other in the "body of Christ" (1 Cor 12), sharing a "common union" and "communion" one with another in the church.

THE HEAD OF THE CHURCH

Jesus Christ is the undisputed "head of the church" and, said Beza, has "no need of any Successor (for he is God living eternally) nor any Vicar or Lieutenant for we have all his will by writing." Beza means here the Scriptures convey Christ's will as the authority and guide for the church (see John 15:15; 2 Tim 3:16–17). Being God, Jesus Christ is "ever present himself in the midst of the Church by his infinite power." Christ will never depart from the church, as he promised (Matt 28:20; John 14:16). This is a promise no one else—a "Vicar or Lieutenant"—can make.

Jesus Christ governs the church by the Holy Spirit. The Spirit is God with God's people and the Spirit is the means by which the church hears and follows the Christ's will for the church. But this does not happen "automatically"! That is, the Spirit uses humans as "instruments."[4] Beza refers to the image Paul used about those who "plant" and those who "water" in regard to the spread of the gospel and thus the means the Spirit uses to govern and guide the church (1 Cor 3:5—4:1; 2 Cor 5:19–20). The Spirit also "distributes His gifts and graces diversely, how, when and to whom it seems good to Him, for the maintenance and government

3. Beza, *Briefe and Pithie Summe*, 80.

4. Beza, *Briefe and Pithie Summe*, 80.

of the entire body of the church (1 Cor 12:7ff.; Eph. 4:10–12) in which He wills all things to be done by good order and policy" (1 Cor 14:40).

Jesus Christ as head of the church is not remote, not far-removed from the communion of saints which constitute his body and are his people to do his will and work in the world. The Holy Spirit is with the church, using its members to carry out the purposes of Jesus Christ to whom all in the church look as the great head of the church. When it comes to discerning truly whether an assembly is a true or false church, Beza indicates that "the mark of the true church is the preaching of the lively Word of the Son of God, as it was revealed to the prophets and apostles, and by them declared to the world. This comprehends consequently the sacraments and the administration of ecclesiastical discipline as God has ordained it. For there is no other Word of God, nor any other way to preach it" (5.7; 88).[5]

MARKS AND MEMBERS OF THE CHURCH

These three "marks of the church" are consistent with what was emphasized in the later Reformed tradition. John Calvin had named two "marks of the church": the preaching of the word of God and the right administration of the sacraments—Baptism and the Lord's Supper. But others, like Beza, went on to signal that the exercise of ecclesiastical or church discipline is a third mark. The church is concerned to see that its members live lives that are consistent with what

---

5. References in this form are to chapter and section of Beza, *Briefe and Pithie Summe* (1565). Again, Beza wrote that "the preaching of the word of God is the only necessary means to salvation, for those which be within age of discretion" (4.35). He also said that "faith comes by hearing, and hearing comes by the preaching of the Word of God." See *Sermons sur l'historie de la resurrection*, 507, cited in Manetsch, *Calvin's Company of Pastors*, 167.

God wills and is revealed in the gospel of Jesus Christ. This means that, at points, the church must take actions to insure a conformity of a person's life with what God requires. Thus various forms of church discipline can be instituted—in the most extreme instances, even excommunication.

In asking, "Who are the True Members of the Church" (5.8), it is faith that is the primary marker (John 8:47; 17:17–20). Beza wrote: "Those have faith who receive the only Savior Jesus Christ, as has been said (John 14:1; 1 John 4:1–3, 15), flying from sin, following righteousness, i.e., who love and fear the true and eternal God only, and their neighbors according to the Word of God, without turning or swerving either to the right hand or to the left" (5.8). This does not mean Christians are "perfect" or sinless. But, there is a "great difference" between those in whom sin reigns fully; and those "in whom there are yet but remnants of sin" (Rom 6:12–13; 2 Cor 7:1; 1 John 3:8–9). Christians in the church strive against the flesh, evil, and sin (Rom 4:7–25; Gal 5:16–18). Those who struggle against sin are "those who are of the true church."

If one asks whether a church is a true or false church, Beza's answer is that while on earth, the "wheat and the chaff" will exist together (5.7; see Matt 3:12). The visible church will consist of those who genuinely have faith in Jesus Christ; and those who don't. There are those who are outside the church and those who are inside the church. But there are also "those who are of the church; and of those who are not of the church, although they are in the church" (5.7).

POWER AND AUTHORITY OF THE CHURCH

The power and authority of the church consists of one word: obedience. This is the obedience the church owes to its "only Spouse Jesus Christ, as to GOD, and to give service to Jesus Christ (Luke 1:74; 1 Peter 1:14). This consists of the members being ordained to aid one another" (1 Cor 12:4–11; Matt 25:15; 5.10).

Beza discussed the church's power and authority of the church in relation to church councils. He is very critical of the actions of the Roman Catholic Church and its head, the bishop of Rome or the pope (5.11–22).

The "universal church" is "an assembly of all the churches (as far as may be) gathered or assembled together" (5.11). This may be called a "general counsel" (see Acts 15). We "doubt not," wrote Beza, that "the Lord is among those who are lawfully called in his name, as he has promised, although they were but two or three" (Matt 18:20). Nor do we doubt that God "governs with greater power in the greater company of his church which he governs by his Holy Spirit" (Acts 15:8, 28).

While ideally, according to Beza, a Christian magistrate should call for a General Council, if the magistrate is not a believer, pastors have authority to call a council and should do so "without ambition or disorder," as seen in the book of Acts (5.13). In ancient church councils, the bishop of Rome did not have special honor and did not call a church council. So Beza believed the pope should have no authority to call and preside over a council. Instead, "the general council" should "set aside all ambition, and take those means which shall be most easy to find, among those who seek the glory of God only. Those ought to proceed and be chief" who are found to be the most suitable "without respect to see [power or authority in a church position] or throne" (5.16).

Church councils should be led by those who seek the "glory of God" in and through the council. Thus "the lawful councils ought to be assembled, without respect to any thing, except only to the honor of God and the edification of the church" (5.17). Councils ought never to "make any new article of our faith." They should neither be "adding nor diminishing to the substance of the word of Jesus Christ." It is never lawful for any person or church body to add to or take from "that doctrine, contained in the Holy Scripture."

Church councils do not meet to "establish and confirm the Scriptures, which are grounded and established upon the eternal truth of God, and shall continue forever; but to confirm themselves by the Scriptures against Satan and his adherents. So then, we believe the holy church, not as the foundation of the Scriptures, but grounded upon the doctrine of the Scriptures, which be pure and the only truth." So, St. Paul was right to call the church the "pillar and ground of the truth" (1 Tim 3:15). Any assembly which swerves or deviates from this "foundation" (Gal 1:8; Col 1:23; 2:10, 18–19), a "false church," and "a whoorish church" which "hears the voice of a stranger" and is not "content with the voice of her spouse" (Rom 7:3–4; John 10:3–5).

Church discipline should be enacted and ordinances established that are "profitable and very appropriate and necessary" (5.20). But, said Beza: "the purest simplicity is the best, and the more Jesus Christ is plainly and simply declared, the more it is agreeable to his word." So the addition of ceremonies—as by the Roman Catholic Church are additions to Scriptures which, said Beza, promoted superstition and idolatry (5.19, 20).

OFFICES IN THE CHURCH

Jesus Christ has ordained four "offices" or ways of serving him in the church (5.23–28). One has the "charge to teach"; another "to distribute the ecclesiastical goods"; a third to "govern the spiritual affairs," which are ecclesiastical ordinances and discipline; and the fourth to serve in respect to "the public affairs of this life," as well as "generally to maintain the tranquility of the whole church, with the power of the sword" (5.23).

Teacher in the church. The first office in the church is Teacher. Here there are five ways ("degrees") teachers have functioned: apostle, prophet, and evangelist—which were found only at the beginning of the church, when God "established the kingdom" of the "new covenant . . . throughout the world"; and pastor and "doctor" (teacher)—which continue to function in the present time of the church.

1. **Pastors** have four functions. Pastors are to be focused on doctrine and prayer—including blessing of Christian marriages, and the administration of the sacraments. Since faith, created by the Holy Spirit, is the only means by which to enter the kingdom of heaven, the preaching of the gospel (along with administration of the sacraments) is where declarations of deliverance from sin, death, and the power of the devil are found (Acts 26:18; Isa 61:1). The preaching function of pastors as the "keys of the kingdom" is central.

It is clearly God alone (5.20) who opens or shuts the doors to the kingdom of heaven, and draws people into faith and gives forgiveness of sins (Mark 2:7). But God is served by persons to "declare his word, and minister his Sacraments" (1 Cor 4:1; 2 Cor 5:20). They function as "trunks" or "conduits" through whom God "distills and powers his trace, into the hearts of his elect" (5.27). This is why such "excellent titles and testimonies have been attributed to the faithful ministers of the Gospel" (Matt 25:21; Acts 26:18). "Ministers of Jesus Christ," wrote Beza, are "distributors of the secrets of God."

There are also "false pastors who are not able or fit to execute the office and charge" given by God (5.28). They do not faithfully expound the "word of God, either changing, putting to, or diminishing it." Instead, they "declare their own fantasies or other persons' traditions instead of the word of God." All such persons, said Beza, are declared to be "false pastors and ministers of Satan, and not of God."

2. **Deacons** are those who minister by distributing "ecclesiastical goods." Hearkening back to the early church in Jerusalem where seven persons were chosen to minister or serve (Gr. *diakonos*) the poor and distribute the church's goods to those in need. Several different classifications of deacons, "sub-deacons," and "minor orders" are mentioned by Beza to meet the needs of the church and its ministries of service (5.30–31).

3. **Elders** or Presbyters were the office in the church whose ministries were in "spiritual jurisdiction" (5.32). Their jurisdiction did not lie in "worldly and temporal things, but altogether in those things which concern the conscience." In this, the elders were "fully distinct from the office of a civil magistrate."

The ministries of elders in ecclesiastical jurisdiction had "one end, that is to say, that all the body of the Church in general, and every member of the same in particular, be preserved and edified in doctrine and well-doing according to the will and word of God" (5.33). This can continue through "good laws and in the good observation of the same." These laws are either "touching the doctrine of salvation generally" concerning the duties which persons "owe to God and their neighbors, or concerning the discipline ['regiment'] or manner of doing, which every one ought to observe in his charge or office." Or, these laws concern the "discipline and regulations which are required, that all things be done in good order, required that all things may be done in good order" according to the "authority of the body of the church." The church must administer discipline or punishment against those who "offend" in observing the church's jurisdiction (5.33). The duties of elders are to "watch, that the Church which is committed to them, be governed by good order, according to the rule of the gospel, and that the ecclesiastical laws and ordinances, either universal or particular, be maintained and executed diligently, according to their charge" (5.34). In sum, elders are to insure "the orders of the church may be maintained with discipline. And above all things," wrote Beza: "let the word of God be diligently and sincerely preached, with the sacraments truly ministered, with ecclesiastical goods well governed, and all things well ordered."

Church discipline is to be carried out by the church, not by using "imprisonments, nor inducements with money, nor corporal pains" (5.40). Rather, the church's discipline is "only with the pure word of God."

Discipline may need to emerge for three causes: false doctrine, bad morals, or offenses against the church's order as determined by "ecclesiastical law."

Through all phases of church discipline, church leaders needed spiritual discernment so they could apply fitting measures of rigor and gentleness. The goal was the repentance and ultimately the restoration of the sinner. Beza once noted that wise pastors need "not only to discern the illness, but also the situation and disposition of the patient, looking for the best medicine to prescribe, preaching the Law to the hardened, and the gospel of grace to those despairing. In brief, let us always condemn the sin, but try to save the sinner."[6]

---

6. Beza, *Sermons sur l'histoire*, 129–30, cited in Manetsch, *Calvin's Company of Pastors*, 189.

The most severe step in church discipline is excommunication. Beza wrote that this is "a sentence whereby the ecclesiastical Seniors [elders] after lawful knowledge of the cause, do declare in the name and authority of God and his holy word, that such or such, one or many be justly excluded and separated from the company or communion of the Saints (1 Cor 5) that is to say the Church of God, and by consequence are delivered to Satan, for inasmuch as without the Church there is no salvation. Yet this is not to continue for ever, but so long as they continue unreformed, and until they have satisfied for the slander or offense given" (5.41).

Excommunication emerges from the authority of God's word. Beza believed "such a power is not grounded upon man, for man hath no manner of power over the soul, but by the authority of God, who uses them in the Church as organs and instruments by whom he speaks, and therefore it is not to be doubted, but such sentences be ratified and confirmed in heaven" (5.41). "Nevertheless," Beza said, "the Church ought after lawful satisfaction, to receive him again who has been cast out, that is to save, if afterward he shall satisfy to the Church, and make amends for the public offense, according to the ordinance of the Church and sufficient proofs had of true amendment, as far as man may judge."

Excommunication can be exacted in varying degrees. Sometimes, a person may be excommunicated from participating in the Lord's Supper; or face a gentler punishment. All such instances are the mutual decisions of the body of church elders. No power of excommunication is given to an individual person. Beza believed that "this power of excommunication promised by Christ is to be exercised by neither a single bishop nor the entire congregation but by the senate of elders."[7]

7. Maruyama, *Ecclesiology of Beza*, 31. In this, Maruyama notes,

These church actions should not be carried out impulsively or rashly. For "the true ecclesiastical eldership cannot and may not use it at their wills, since we see that all men are subject to many infirmities. But this power is limited and appointed by the Word of God" (5.41). The end or purpose of excommunication as ordained by God, in Beza's view was:

> First that the church of God should be as pure as might be possible, and that there might be no occasion to think, that it should be a refuge or den of the wicked (1 Cor 5). Second for fear that the infected should not defile those who were whole. Third if it were possible that the sinner might be brought home that the sinner might be brought home to the flock again. It follows then that this punishment must be applied and used for to edify, as may be expedient, and that there be good care is taken, least they confound the sinner by too much heaviness and sorrow, when he gives a sign of repentance. Instead they should mitigate the punishment when need shall require it. (5.41)

Beza "insisted that excommunicated persons should be welcomed—indeed encouraged—to attend public preaching services, because it was by hearing God's Word that even the most hardened sinners might be brought to repentance. And was not repentance 'the principle goal of excommunication' in the first place?"[8]

Civil Magistrates. Those who rule in governments are instituted by God (Rom 13:1). Their purpose is to perform and execute civil and temporal affairs so that "their subjects may live in peace" (5.42). To do this, there is need for "taxes

---

Beza agreed with Calvin.

8. Manetsch, *Calvin's Company of Pastors*, 194.

and subsidies" to come to them (Matt 22:15–22) and they are empowered to use the "sword which God has given them" (Rom 13:4) to preserve the countries committed to them. Civil authorities must also defend and maintain "good laws and the punishment of evil and wicked doers."

Magistrates who provide for the "peace and concord of subjects" do this for the purpose that this peace and concord will bring the "honor and glory of God" and so all persons may "live not only in a certain civil honesty, but also with piety and true worship of God" (1 Tim 2:1–2). Magistrates should see that the laws of a land which are used and carried out are "conformable to the will of God" so religion is "perfect and holy" and that "all the Church is ordered according to the word of God, forbidding and punishing, as cases require."

Since there is no faithful person exempt from obedience owed to Jesus Christ in his church—whether it be a king, prince, or subject—so, said Beza: "there is none from the greatest to the least who does not owe voluntary obedience to the Magistrate, as ordained by God" (5.43; Rom 13; Titus 3:1; 1 Peter 2:13–14). Obedience is owed, even if the magistrate is a tyrant. But there is one exception. That is, obedience is not to be given to a magistrate if that person commands one to "do things which are against God's word." In this case (as the apostles said), one must obey God rather than humans, for otherwise we "extol men above God" (Acts 4:19–20).

Thus it is "not rebellion to disobey Princes" when they would cause us "to do that which God forbids or to defend or forbid that which God commands." Here a middle way must be kept ("a meane kepte") that magistrates do not "pass or exceed their vocation." The apostles did not obey those who wanted to prohibit them from preaching Jesus Christ. Beza rejected those who thought these views would make persons "seditious and disobedient to kings and superiors." "On the contrary," Beza argued, "the gospel establishes their power" (5.43).[9]

The Church's Ministry in Preaching and Teaching

Theodore Beza was considered a pastor in Geneva from 1559–1605. He was Professor of Theology in the Geneva Academy, where pastors were trained from 1559–1599. Beza's wide and deep scholarship was all offered in service to the church—locally in Geneva; but ecumenically—to the church of Jesus Christ throughout the world.[10] His own activities reflected aspects of the church's ministry carried out through the church's authority and the offices in the church through which the "company of the faithful" gave glory to God and served God in the world.

Preaching and Teaching. After the death of John Calvin, Beza was the chief minister of the Genevan church, assuming leadership roles with the Company of Pastors. In this, Beza "played a crucial role in preserving Calvin's theological legacy and promoting international Calvinism."[11]

Since one of the theological marks of the church was the preaching of the word of God (see above), Beza was active in preaching. He preached more than three thousand sermons in Geneva's St. Pierre church (though only eighty-seven sermons survive). In this, Beza—and his other pastor colleagues in Geneva—were maintaining the true nature of the church as the context where the Word of God is

9. Maruyama says that Beza "takes a typically traditional view and discourages any attempts of resistance to the magistracy" (Maruyama, *Ecclesiology of Theodore Beza*, 35).

10. Beza, as well as Calvin, "warned would-be ministers against becoming bookworms, aloof from the problems and needs of their parishioners" (Manetsch, *Calvin's Company of Pastors*, 133).

11. Manetsch, *Encyclopedia of Protestantism*, 1:221.

proclaimed in preaching. As Beza said in a sermon: "The Holy Spirit is the only doctor, having here spoken by the lips of the Master, as he speaks in his church by the lips of his faithful servants."[12] The ministry of the word of God was carried out in the church by the work of the Holy Spirit who spoke to the church through the sermons of faithful pastors and preachers who proclaimed the word.

Those who preach and teach in the church have the responsibility of being faithful interpreters of Scripture. They were to proclaim the message of the Bible so the church and its members can be established and built up in Christian faith.[13] Their preaching was to covey biblical teachings. In this, Geneva's preachers followed Calvin in his "simple, doctrinal style of expository preaching" which "became the model for homiletics in Geneva and among French Protestants during the generation after his death."[14] Beza urged this biblical fidelity to a former student, Louis Courant, in a letter after Courant had begun a pastoral ministry in France:

> Be on your guard and in constant care, both as
> to the doctrine that you have the responsibility
> to proclaim in its purity and entirety, as well as
> to the way you present it to your flock. Beware of

12. From Beza's 1593, Sermons sur la Resurrection, sermon 9, translated in Wright, *Our Sovereign Refuge*, 257.

13. A way in which sound biblical interpretation was institutionalized for Geneva's pastors was through the weekly Congregation, established by Calvin and William Farel in 1536. This was modeled after Zwingli's Prophezei in Zurich to provide "a regular setting in which ministers, professors, and interested laypeople could study and discuss the contents of Scripture together" (Manetsch, *Calvin's Company of Pastors*, 134).

14. Manetsch, *Calvin's Company of Pastors*, 164. Beza noted that "in practice, Calvin's sermons were becoming a kind of new handbook for French pastors." McKee, *Pastoral Ministry*, 563. See this magisterial book's chapter 6: "Calvin the Preacher of Geneva." Cf. Manetch, *Company of Pastors*, ch. 6: "The Ministry of the Word."

> polluting the holiness of true doctrine, either by indulging in vain and curious speculations and subtleties directly contrary to its simple purity, or by using a flowery eloquence that is entirely at odds with the serious and sound . . . simplicity of the prophets and apostles, a style that is truly divine and heavenly.[15]

In short, Beza believed that in "the ordinary administration of the Word," Jesus Christ "also presents his entire self to us, to be received as by the hand of our faith."[16]

Worship and the Psalms. Worship was central to the church's life and ministry. Not only was public worship where the word of God was proclaimed and the sacraments were rightly administered (the description of the church) but it was where God was glorified and the congregation could express their honor, worship, and commitment to God, their Creator and Sustainer. Church worship was where ordinary Genevans could be helped to understand how all aspects of their lives could confirm to their Christian faith, in its Reformed expression. The church's sacraments—Baptism and the Lord's Supper—were administered in public services of worship.

Besides preaching and administering the sacraments, Theodore Beza contributed to the church's worship. Beza joined with the French poet Clément Marot in setting the Psalms into verse. These were joined with the music written by Louis Bourgeois and Pierre Davantes to provide the "Genevan Psalter" used for congregational singing in worship. Careful structuring of worship to indicate what Psalm or

---

15. Manetsch, *Calvin's Company of Pastors*, 164. Beza indicated pastors needed to relate the word of God to the congregation: "It is necessary to apply the medicine to the patients, for otherwise preaching would be without fruit" (168).

16. Cited in Manetsch, *Company of Pastors*, 168.

part of a Psalm should be sung at which service made it possible for all Psalms to be sung over the succession of weekday and Sunday worship services over seventeen weeks.

By 1567, "the entire set of 150 Psalms had been versified and set to music."[17] The Psalms, as holy Scripture and as the words God wanted conveyed in the Bible, were considered the appropriate words to be sung use in worship services. By "binding the Psalter, the Genevan catechism, prayers, and orders of service together with the Bible allowed Genevans to purchase a multipurpose worship resource that could be used equally well at church and at home during family devotions."[18]

QUESTIONS FOR DISCUSSION

1. Why is it important for Beza to present a strong and vigorous doctrine of the church in relation to God's election and the salvation given in Jesus Christ?

2. What are implications for the church when it acknowledges Jesus Christ is the Head of the church?

3. Why is it important to be honest in recognizing the church is not composed of "perfect" people, but of forgiven sinners?

4. In what ways do you find that worshiping God in the church strengthens and deepens your Christian faith?

17. Maag, *Lifting Hearts to the Lord*, 92. Maag's book is a very helpful resource.

18. Maag, *Lifting Hearts to the Lord*, 92. The Genevan Psalter had wide usage in Reformed churches internationally for several centuries.

8

WORD AND SACRAMENTS

THE WORD

THE PREACHED WORD OF God is the word of God. That brief and profound sentiment resounds through Reformed theology like a church bell echoes through a small Bavarian valley. Beza believed it too, and taught it to his students and his congregations.

And yet, the preached word was not of equal reliability as the written word, which is why the Reformers and their heirs always were careful to distinguish, in their doctrinal expositions, the written word of Scripture from the preached word of the sermon. Indeed, the architecture of Reformed Churches illustrated the fact that the written word was qualitatively different than the preached word, since they made use of one pulpit for preaching and a different pulpit for Scripture reading. This "divided chancel" made clear to those sitting in pews and standing in aisles that when they heard Scripture read, they were hearing God's unmixed word; and when they listened to the sermon preached, they were hearing God making use of a fallible and sometimes mistaken human vessel.

The preached word of God is the word of God. But it fails to achieve the same level of reliability and perfection as the Scriptures themselves. You can trust the preacher, until you hear something the Bible does not say. In which case you should most certainly not trust the words of the preacher instead of the words of Scripture.

The Bible, the Scriptures, have already been examined in terms of Beza's theology, above in chapter 2. Here our consideration will be limited to Beza's understanding of the preached word of God. And more particularly, the preacher of that word.

Ministers of the Gospel

Ministry, and ministers, are, according to Beza, an establishment of Christ himself. He gave the church ministers and they are tasked by him to carry out the ministry to which they are appointed. Ministry is no man-made invention, it is the work and will of God.

Ministers are to govern the church under the headship of Christ himself. This governance takes place in two respects; ministers are to do the work of ministering to the church, and they are to "knit the saints together."[1] No calling, Beza notes, curiously, is perpetual nor is any calling limited to a set span of time. In other words, Beza believed that ministerial calling was neither a lifetime appointment nor limited to, say, a year or ten. Each calling was specific, and particular in both time and place, as determined by God and by God alone.

1. All references and citations in this subsection are drawn from Beza, *Propositions and Principles*, 332ff., which confer.

The names given to those who are called to this ministry are sometimes elders, sometimes deacons; yet at other times the general signification also applies to specific offices within the church—in the offices of the pastor and the deacon. But Beza also asserts that three of the names given to ministers were for the beginning of the church only and that the names given to two are to abide until the end of time. That is, apostles, evangelists, and prophets were "appointed for the planting of the Church throughout the world" and once accomplished, those offices ceased. Pastors and deacons, however, remain offices within the church till the consummation.

Pastors and deacons, Beza continues, are ordained by men to serve in a particular congregation. Within the ranks of the pastors are the doctors, the teachers, whose task it is to teach "the doctrine of true religion" by faithfully interpreting Scripture, defending the faith against adversaries, and governing ecclesiastical schools. Fascinating, indeed, is the notion that theological education is done by the doctors, themselves pastors, yet with more expertise than other pastors.

The tasks of the pastors themselves are threefold: preaching and teaching Scripture both publicly and privately and admonishing and correcting their congregation; administering the sacraments; and holding public prayers.

The elders, in their particular work, are to oversee the correction and moral instruction of members of the congregation who have erred or strayed. And, if necessary, they must see to it that sinners are not allowed to perish, but must instead be humbled, and even shamed if needed, so that they might return to the proper course of life.

In short, doctors teach, pastors preach and pray, and elders correct, chasten, shame, and humble the wayward. These are their duties.

Deacons, on the other hand, are those charged with receiving and distributing alms and the administration of the other goods of the church for the well being of the poor and the widows. No one can assume any of these responsibilities, Beza insists, unless he has been properly called after a serious examination of his life, his morals, and his beliefs, by the church to which he is to be appointed. It is, Beza says, unlawful for any person not properly examined and ordained to act in any ministerial capacity.

And these ordinations must be carried out by properly ordained doctors, pastors, elders, and deacons, since they have the oversight of the flock and must be responsible for its well being. The magistrate, if a Christian, may also have a say in who is ordained, as well as the congregation itself. Then, and only then, may the pastors lay hands on the candidate for ordination.

And then, interestingly, Beza laments the failure of the church to see to it that only properly ordained and examined men have taken up church leadership.

> We see that is has often come to pass, as was expressly foretold by the Spirit of God, that the public ministry is, for the most part, not in the hands of careful shepherds, but instead is in the hands of forlorn spoiler and wasters of the Church; Antichrist himself sits in the very Temple of God.

Such dire circumstances allow God, of his good grace, to raise up preachers without church appointments to call the church back to its proper course and congregations to replace their evil pastors with ones suitable to the calling of Christ. This leads Beza to his next point: what happens when a church has a false minister and what can be done about it?

False Ministers of the Gospel

Setting side by side the true minister with the false, Beza believes that the true might be more clearly known and easily recognized. The false, then, are characterized by their ordination from the hierarchy of the Roman Catholic Church. It instantly, then, becomes clear that Beza is not interested so much in distinguishing the good pastor from the bad, but the good pastor (the properly called, ordained, and appointed Reformed pastor) from the bad (the Catholic priest).

The priesthood of Rome is rooted in the calling of the Vatican, and the appointment by the Vatican of the priest. These priests are "counterfeit"[2] because they are not properly called by God, but man. Counterfeit priests naturally perform counterfeit, and false, ministries.

The bishop of Rome, Beza insists, has usurped the other bishops and has set in order a ministry of man and not God.

> The Apostles were of equal authority and power amongst themselves, as it appears in the Commandment of Christ who appointed them.

The basis of Roman authority is a man. In Beza's estimation this is a denial of Christ himself and the order established by him for the conduct of the ministry and the calling of the minister. The destruction of the foundation established by Christ is the basis of the destruction of the church under Roman authority.

Beza makes the further observation that there is absolutely no need for any supposed or putative apostolic succession since the function of the apostles ceased when

---

2. For this section, cf. Beza, *Propositions and Principles*, 339ff.

they died and the ministry which followed was the result of God's calling and not human appointment.

Next, he goes into a great deal of detail concerning the Roman offices of cardinals, bishops, archbishops, prelates, curates and the rest, calling them what all should know them to be:

> . . . and ought to be accounted, the most ugly
> brood of Satan begotten by him in the last days
> for the defense of that strumpet [the Pope].

The Reformers were not shy about utilizing *ad hominem* arguments when it helped them make a point.

Beza also denounces the practice of elevating one local church above other local churches. He sees this as simply a prideful attempt to elevate one minister and one ministry above another and this has no basis in Scripture itself nor in the calling of Christ. This happened because the church adopted the pattern of governance of the Roman Empire and, like the Israelites before them, rejected the authority of God to replace it with the authority of a human king. Indeed, Beza would prefer the church be a theocracy to its being a monarchy (which is exactly what he saw it to be under Rome).

False ministers, then, are humanly appointed men working for a monarch (the pope) in a government (not a true church) to further the goals of the king (not God). Beza will address the authority of the true Minster in due course, having delineated the basis of false ministers, who have their authority only from man, and not from God.

The Minister's Only Authority

If the authority of the pastor does not derive from the supposed Apostolic Succession, as the Catholic Church asserted and insisted, and upon which its entire "government" was built, then where did the authority of the minister, and conjointly, the church, originate and what was its scope and legitimate arena? Beza has an answer, but he first wishes to insist that the authority of the church and its ministers is *purely* spiritual and is severed from the authority and power of the magistrate (or secular government).

Secondly, Beza asserts that the authority of the minister and the church are administrative, not sovereign. What he means by this is that the church and its pastors can only provide spiritual guidance, and they cannot enforce or coerce or otherwise manipulate or control the lives of any persons (save through the remedy of removing the unrepentant from the community of faith by excommunication; a topic to which we will return shortly). There is only one Lord of the church, and that is the Lord.

Having delineated the limitations of ministerial/ churchly authority, Beza describes the authority of the pastor as directed both against the kingdom of Satan and for the house of God. Authority, properly exercised, combats the devil and upbuilds the kingdom of God.

> This whole power consists in three points;
> namely in teaching, in establishing regulations,
> and in censuring the wandering.[3]

Beza then enters into a description of each of these three aspects of the authority of the church and its pastors. In sum, everything the church and its minsters does should be done both to the glory of God and to the edification of the church.

The authority of the church is metaphorically described, in Beza's estimation, of the "keys." By making this assertion Beza is stripping the Roman papacy of its claim to

---

3. Beza, *Propositions and Principles*, 357.

be the sole inheritor of the authority of Christ and handing, literally, the keys over to the church and its pastors. This is, frankly, an astonishingly brilliant move as it simultaneously denudes the papacy of any power and establishes the authority of the Reformed faith.

For its part, in relation to the authority of the church, the magistrate must maintain its own proper jurisdiction and not assume the responsibilities of the church any more than the church is to assume the responsibilities of the government. But more on this in the next chapter.

Now the task at hand is to examine Beza's views on church discipline. To which we now turn our gaze.

The Minister and Church Discipline

Since the church is comprised of human beings, there are bound to be problems. These problems can be personal in nature (sin) and they can be corporate (church fights, etc.). Beza was naturally aware of these facts and so he turns to the way in which the church must address these problems.

But bluntly, sin must be purged from the body of Christ. Individual sins and corporate sins cannot remain because they endanger the entire community of faith. One of the chief tasks of the pastor is to ensure the integrity of the body of Christ and that means taking a lead in purging it of sin.

Practically, then, this means that when problems arise or sins are exposed, censure must be administered. Especially in terms of problems causing divisions within the community of faith.

> This censure is rightly administered when those in authority bring the parties together and patiently hear them and their witnesses and the whole controversy then must be decided in

reverence of God, without prejudice or favoritism, as the Apostle Paul teaches.[4]

The same procedures are to be followed with schismatics and heretics. When, though, private sins are the subject of censure, the sinning brother or sister must be urged to repent and to be restored to full communion. In love. But if they refuse, then their obstinance must see to their expulsion. Matthew 18 is the key text for Beza on these matters:

> Moreover if your brother sins against you, go and tell him his fault between you and him alone. If he hears you, you have gained your brother. But if he will not hear, take with you one or two more, that "by the mouth of two or three witnesses every word may be established." And if he refuses to hear them, tell it to the church. But if he refuses even to hear the church, let him be to you like a heathen and a tax collector. Assuredly, I say to you, whatever you bind on earth will be bound in heaven, and whatever you loose on earth will be loosed in heaven. (Matt 18:15–18 NKJV)

When censure is applied, it is applied in the forms of admonition, suspension from the Lord's Supper, and excommunication, until repentance is public and demonstrable. When a person is excommunicated, Beza asserts, they must also be shunned. This shunning is exercised in the hope that the shunned will feel intense shame and thus be moved to repentance.

The act of confession and public repentance is to be made before the pastors and elders. All of which is to make every member of the church fit to take part in the sacraments. To which we now turn.

4. Beza, *Propositions and Principles*, 364. And so throughout this section see *Propositions and Principles*, 364ff.

SACRAMENTS

Naturally, when Beza discusses theological matters, he discusses the sacraments. Sacramental issues had a long and troubled history in the Reformation. From the early argument between Luther and Zwingli through the ongoing attempts to come to some sort of agreement between Calvin and Bullinger and Bucer, the matter was never resolved to the satisfaction of all parties. Lutherans held to their views and the Reformed vacillated between Zwingli's "memorialism" and Calvin's more nuanced "both/and" understanding of the presence of Christ in the elements of the Last Supper.

Beza was compelled, as was everyone else, to make a statement on his beliefs concerning the issue so that his enemies and his friends would know who he was and what he believed and in which tribe he belonged.

Beza's overview begins with a note that God not only saves, but gives those saved certain assurances of their relationship with him. These are the sacraments, which provide assurance of faith. How do you know you believe? You have taken part in the sacraments. These sacraments combine the sign and the thing signified, rooting in the heart of the believer and offering certainty of salvation.[5] After lengthily describing how assurance is provided by the sacraments, without even yet naming them, which he will do in the section to follow, Beza sagely concludes:

> The preaching of the word may be offered by itself to the Church, without the Sacraments, but the Sacraments are never to be administered without the word preached. This because the word affects just one of our senses (hearing) the Sacraments are experienced by several of them,

5. Beza, *Propositions and Principles*, 246ff. for this section.

especially the sense of sight. This is why they are more effectual means of apprehending Christ when they are properly administered.

The Catholic Church asserted the existence of seven sacraments, baptism, confirmation, Eucharist, penance, anointing of the sick, matrimony, and holy orders. Each of the Reformers rejected the sacramental nature of five of these and held to the existence of just two authentic sacraments: Baptism and the Lord's Supper. Beza discusses this topic next.

The Number of the Sacraments

Beza gets directly to the point on this matter:[6]

> The Sacraments of the New Testament are those which Christ has instituted into his Church, which are to remain in place until his second coming. Of this, there are only two; baptism and the Supper of the Lord. By the former we are received into the Church and by the latter we are nourished and sustained in the Church.

There are two, and only two sacraments that should be and are functional in the Christian church. This may seem common knowledge among Protestant and Reformed Christians today, but in the sixteenth century it was truly revolutionary.

The importance of the sacraments in Roman Catholic theology in the period of the Reformation, and before, is hard to overstate. Sacraments communicated salvation, i.e., they aided in the process of being saved. They granted it. They were the means by which it could be achieved.

To be sure, the Catholic Church then and always believed that salvation was by faith through grace. But in

---

6. Beza, *Propositions and Principles*, 259ff. for this and what follows in this segment.

contrast to the Reformers, they believed there were things believers could do to help the process of salvation along. They could be baptized, partake of the Lord's Supper, get married, receive holy unction, join the priesthood, etc. These didn't bring salvation fully, but they sure helped.

The Reformers were more strictly minded regarding human participation in the process of salvation. They believed that only Jesus could bring salvation but they also believed that the sacraments were marks of faith and grace rather than means of faith and grace.

Beza spends the rest of the present subdivision rejecting the reasons that the Catholic Church deems other actions "sacramental." He now addresses the two sacraments which he, and the remainder of the Reformed, accepted.

Baptism

In the theology of Theodore Beza, baptism is the Christian replacement of circumcision. Baptism is the first of the two New Testament sacraments and is a "dipping into water and a taking out thereof."[7] This signifies, Beza continues, the dipping of the believer into the blood of Jesus.

Baptism is "lawfully administered" when administered by the church and its properly ordained clergy, and done in the name of the Father, the Son, and the Holy Spirit, whether by dipping or by sprinkling.

> It is not greatly material whether the person that is to be baptized is wholly immersed under the water or whether the water is only sprinkled either on his head or face. Any "washing" that is not done in the name of the Father, Son, and Holy Spirit or done without water is meaningless and pointless.

7. Beza, *Propositions and Principles*, 263ff., throughout the section.

Baptism in its simplicity is the sacramental sign God intended. In this simplicity it is sufficient and additions to it either by means of tradition or novelty are neither appropriate nor proper. For instance, the application of spittle to the baptized person or the use of candles during the ceremony are completely unnecessary and added by human will and not divine command. Nor is exorcism as an addition to the Sacrament proper.

Again, as noted above, only pastors may baptize. It is a "grievous error" to allow non-ordained men, or women, to baptize. Baptism must also be performed at the church.

> The proper goal of baptism is that by this solemn and holy action we might be known by the testimony of men and angels to be among the number of the visible church, and that also by baptism the adoption of the elect might receive the assurance of the sealing of the Holy Spirit in their hearts.

Baptism, for Beza, is the pledge or promise of salvation. What of the second sacrament? How does Beza understand the Lord's Supper?

The Lord's Supper

Beza launches immediately into a precise definition of the Lord's Supper:[8]

> The Supper is the final Sacrament of the New Testament—a public act of the Christian Church whereat the bread being broken is given to be eaten and the wine poured out so that all assembled may drink it; all of which represents the body of Christ being delivered to death and his blood being shed in order to seal those in

8. Beza, *Propositions and Principles*, 273ff.

> covenant with God; and they are given to the
> faithful who are able to examine themselves;
> and they are spiritually received in faith for the
> reasons already given.

Beza here asserts several important facts: the Supper is to be received in both kinds (the bread and the wine; these two elements "represent" the body and blood of Christ; the receiving of these elements seals those so doing in covenant with God; they are only to be given to those who are able to "examine themselves" (i.e., they are not to be given to infants or children below the age of sensibility); and most importantly, they are "spiritually received" in faith.

By describing the Supper in this way, Beza is touching on each and every one of the major sticking points concerning the theology of the Supper as they raged across the sixteenth century.

In contrast to the Catholic Church, which allowed only the distribution of the bread to the laity, the wine being reserved to the clergy, Beza sees both given to the worshipping community. Furthermore, in dialogue with everyone, Beza touches on the notion of the "real presence" of Christ in the Supper. No, he insists, the bread and wine are *not* Jesus, they represent Jesus.

Receiving the elements binds recipients in covenant with God. They are no empty symbols, rather, they are powerful reminders of one's relationship with God. Relationships are for those who can assent to them and agree to participate in them. Accordingly, only persons capable of entering into relationships are allowed to take part in the Supper.

And finally, these elements are received spiritually. Their meaning is spiritually centered, not bodily. The focus is not on the material of the Supper but the meaning of the Supper. This refocusing is not a diminishment of the Supper's materials, but their exalting. The are not mere bread and wine, they are the body and blood of Jesus! Not in some crass materialistic way, but in a supremely meaningful spiritual way.

Beza here threads a very narrow path between Calvin and Bullinger and Zwingli and Melanchthon, touching at points with each of them and swerving from them at others, but ever so slightly. Beza's theology of the Supper may well be the high-water mark of the theology of the Eucharist from the sixteenth century and it is fair to say that it has never been surpassed, or eclipsed, for its simplicity, sensibility, and profundity.

The exposition of the doctrine of the Lord's Supper, like the exposition of baptism, and all of the other teachings of the Christian Church which Beza addresses in his many sermons, books, lectures, and debates is aimed at helping regular believers, layfolk, understand the doctrines of their faith with the aim of living better lives of faithfulness to God. Doctrine must result in changed behavior or it serves no authentic purpose.

The word preached, the ministry of the church performed, the sacraments taken and enjoyed and believers edified, encouraged, chastened, corrected, and reformed all resulting in faith lived. Faith itself actually, thoroughly, functionally lived.

QUESTIONS FOR DISCUSSION

1. Do you think when the Bible is preached, the word of God is heard?

2. How many sacraments do you believe should exist in the practice of the church?

3. How important is participating in the sacraments to your own spiritual development?

4. Do you agree with Beza's analysis of the Supper?

5. Do you receive the bread and the wine, or just one in your communion services?

9

THE STATE AND LAST THINGS

THE STATE

THEODORE BEZA WOULD THOROUGHLY agree with John Calvin's assessment of the purpose of the magistracy, or in our terminology, the government, the state:

> The Magistrate is God's vicegerent, the father of his country, the guardian of the laws, the administrator of justice, the defender of the Church.[1]

As was true of the other Reformers of the first and second generations, Beza had little to say about the state. It was simply taken for granted as a reality established by God and it was the duty of every Christian to obey it. Kings, magistrates, judges, were all seen as the voice of God and were expected to be heard as such.

It was this notion that the government was God's second voice, following the church and working in tandem

1. Calvin, *Institutes*, aphorism 92.

with it, that made any notion of the so-called separation of church and state absolutely unthinkable to them. Which, naturally, is why the Anabaptist call to sever the church from the state seemed not only absurd, but actually heretical. God spoke through and used the state. To separate it from the church would be to cut off one of God's hands.

What, then, did Beza have to say about the government? The answer to that question can be found in his already previously mentioned numerous times *Propositions and Principles of Divinity* on pages 380 and following through page 386. It is, it's fair to say, his shortest treatment of any topic in his theological exposition of the Lord's Prayer and the creeds.[2]

Beza begins by noting that human sin is the reason government even has to exist. People are obstinate, and stubborn, and refuse to heed the word of God, so the state must exist in order to corral them in to good, or at least acceptable behavior. The church wields the Word, and the state wields the sword precisely to punish those who refuse to abide by the word. The state, in sum, legislates morality for those who are neither willing to be nor attempting to be moral persons. The state, in Beza's clever phrasing, heals the "untamed and brutish unruliness of men."

This power has resided in the state since the beginning of the world, Beza attests, and has always been the appointee of God. God has always wanted government. God uses government. God ordains government. The word and the sword. The right hand of God and his left. To ensure that humanity is and remains civilized.

Government, Beza believes, was not instituted for the harm of humanity but for its preservation. Indeed, these

2. What follows in this subsection is from Beza, *Propositions and Principles*, 380ff.

appointees are called "Elohim," gods, by Scripture. Or so Beza asserts.

The forms instituted by God of government are two-fold: monarchy, and democracy. Monarchy is the governing of the populace by one while democracy is the governing of the populace by all. At this point in his exposition of the doctrine of the State and its power in the service of the will of God, Beza goes on a bit of a rant against the Anabaptists, writing:

> The Anabaptists are to be detested, who despise all government and speak evil of the superior powers under the pretense of a kind of imagined perfection which doesn't need any sort of the governing of any man. Their nonsense is also frivolous, as they set out to prove that no government is needed because we have Jesus Christ as our Lord and King, by whose Spirit we are led and the Lord exercises through his inward power its influence on the conscience of his children. Thus, they insist, God's children do not need the outward dominion of a Magistrate.[3]

Beza's next remarks, though, are fairly standard given his place in the sixteenth century. He opines that the power of the magistrate extends to making it possible nor only for people to live peacefully, but religiously. The state exists to enable people to live out their Christian faith. Indeed, it is their duty to ensure that their subjects listen to Scripture and follow its teachings.

Magistrates are also required to fulfill their duty, to compel the ecclesiastical authorities to do their job and they are also the people responsible for punishing blasphemers and heretics and to prevent schisms. Anything that attempts to "overthrow the gospel" is in fact their purview.

3. Beza, *Propositions and Principles*, 381–82.

The broad powers of the magistracy in terms of the way Christianity in Beza's day saw the power of the state strikes modern Westerners who live in democratic societies as both odd and oppressive. To appreciate Beza's views fully modern people would need to imagine living in a place where the state fully supported Christianity and even enforced Christian teachings. Compulsory behavior based on the interpretation of Scripture according to the doctrinal teachings of a particular incarnation of Christian belief would be "normal" and any violation of Christian teaching would result in quite severe penalties. That is the world which Beza, and for that matter Luther, Zwingli, Calvin, and everyone alive in Europe in the sixteenth century, knew and inhabited.

Naturally doctrinal questions arose causing various kinds of disagreements. It was, therefore, the duty of the magistrate to assemble an Ecclesiastical Synod so that the pastors and theologians could gather and arrive at an agreement and thus the people receive assurance that all were believing, and practicing, the same things. Differences of opinions were allowed, until they became fractures in the church and thus in society. Then those differences had to be resolved and the party responsible for setting that solution in motion were not the church's leaders but the state's.

Innocence, tranquility, and modesty are the chief concerns of the magistrates and ensuring that the population abides in those virtues is their calling as enforcers of the "second table of the law." To carry out enforcement of Christian ethics, the magistrates are empowered to use the sword.

Put plainly, the power of the sword was reserved to the state and not the church. The church could not execute criminals but the state could. And did. Frequently. Capital punishment was as common in the sixteenth century as imprisonment for serious crimes is today. And the magistrates were in command of the executioners.

To be sure, the church brought charges against those who were criminal but those criminals were then handed over to the state for punishment. Thus, while, for example, Calvin is often accused of killing Servetus, he did not. He could not have done so if he had wanted to. Rather, he presented charges of heresy against Servetus to the Council of Geneva, and the Council rendered the only proper punishment for heresy of death by burning.

Magistrates also bear the responsibility of declaring war, when all other avenues for peace have been exhausted, Beza insists. Again, then, it is improper to assert that Zwingli led Zurich to war against the Catholic Cantons. Instead, he warned the magistrates of the consequences of indecision and the magistrates declared war. It may appear that the cases of Servetus and the Second Kappel War were the direct fault of Calvin and Zwingli, nothing simply could be further from the truth.[4]

To fund their work and their wars, the magistrates are permitted to raise tributes and taxes.

> The annual revenues, furthermore, whereby the Magistrates do maintain the honor and magnificence of their daily lives, things relevant to the dignity of their governmental responsibilities, are to be paid to them.[5]

Beza appears to believe that magistrates should live fairly luxurious lives as befitting their station. And that the

---

4. On Calvin and Servetus, see "*The Servetus Controversy,*" https://calvin.edu/centers-institutes/meeter-center/files/resources-page/TheServetusControversy.pdf. On *Zwingli and the Second Kappel War* see https://blog.nationalmuseum.ch/en/2021/10/the-second-war-of-kappel/.

5. Beza, *Propositions and Principles*, 383–84.

population is required to make sure that they pay taxes and tributes in order not only to fund wars and governmental activities, but to fund luxury for the magistrates. Given that most people were abjectly poor, it is perhaps incredible to modern Christians that the church sided with the state in funding elite lifestyles for the few. And yet the fact that Beza and other theologians gave theological justification for extravagant living for the few made it difficult for average Christians to speak up or speak out or even object publicly to the practice. The poor get poorer and the rich get richer in Beza's world, and the church enabled it.

Laws can be changed, Beza asserts, so long as they do not infringe on the primary purpose of all laws—to enforce the glorification of God, and the betterment of the citizenry (though it seems to have escaped Beza that the betterment of the citizenry really only meant the enrichment of the magistrates and the control of the general population).

The powers of the magistrates are virtually unassailable, for Beza. He notes:

> We hold that it is not lawful in any event for private citizens to rise up against their Magistrates, even if they be the worst of tyrants; for it is a far different thing than refusing to render obedience to impious and unjust laws.[6]

Being disobedient to unjust laws is one thing, but rising up against evil magistrates is another altogether. Beza believes that even evil magistrates are appointed by God for a purpose and that rising against them is rising against the purpose of God himself.

The consequences of his view, which was also held by Luther and Bucer and Calvin and Bullinger and Zwingli and the other Reformers (aside from Hubmaier and Simons

6. Beza, *Propositions and Principles*, 384.

and the other Anabaptists) had horrific consequences in the twentieth century in Germany when the very line of thought Beza expresses here was followed by the German Christians and the supporters in the Church of Adolph Hitler. God appointed him, he must not be attacked.

Doctrinal beliefs always matter because they result in behavior. And behavior can be exceedingly evil, or exceptionally good, depending on the teaching of the faith. Or, in a different way of saying the same thing: what people believe doctrinally matters far more than our secular Western world would like to admit.

Christians, Beza writes, should, of all people, be the least given to contentiousness. They are perfectly within their rights to raise their concerns to the magistrates, but never contentiously and certainly never to the extent that they actually ever disobey, or worse, rise up against them in open rebellion. Even if those magistrates are enemies of true faith! Christians, even then, must avoid any guilt, revenge, guile, and evil intentions.

Those, Beza remarks, who think Christians should never raise concerns with magistrates are wrong, though. Christians may, again, raise those issues. But must, again, be obedient to the decisions of the state.

For all of this the only scriptural justification Beza references is the apostle's "command to pray for all magistrates without exception."

> Therefore I exhort first of all that supplications, prayers, intercessions, and giving of thanks be made for all men, for kings and all who are in authority, that we may lead a quiet and peaceable life in all godliness and reverence. (1 Tim 2:1–2 NKJV)

It is a bit of a stretch to move from prayer to absolute obedience, yet Beza, and the other Reformers, make it.

Interestingly, Beza accuses the Catholic clergy of being rebellious and seditious when it refuses to abide by the rulings of the magistrates. It is up to the magistrates themselves, and the monarchs, to restrain evil government. It is not the place of the people to do so.

There are only two instances where rejecting the order of the magistrates is permissible. Anything they command which hinders the worship of God or love of neighbor can be safely ignored, for the sake of conscience. Whenever the commandments of God and man are at odds, the commandments of God must be obeyed, even if citizens must then suffer the ultimate penalty. Indeed, Beza concludes his discussion of the magistrate, the state, thusly:

> As often as the Magistrate commands anything that is repugnant to the worship which we owe to God or the love which we owe to our neighbor, we cannot yield obedience with a clear conscience. For as often as the commandments of God and men are in direct opposition against one another, we are to observe, forever, this one absolute rule: It is better to obey God than man.

Unfortunately that wasn't the last sentence. He concludes with a bit of a loophole which will ensure the power of the magistrate. Perpetually.

> Yet, no man is to exceed the boundaries of his own calling.

Disobey if you must, but under no circumstances may you attempt to overthrow the state. That is Beza's final note on the relationship of the Christian to the governing authorities. And it had, as noted above, severely dire consequences.

Finally, then, we turn our gaze toward Beza's teachings concerning the Last Things (death, judgment, hell, etc.). All arrive at the end of their journey eventually. What then?

LAST THINGS

The Resurrection of the Flesh

The final pages of Beza's sweeping examination of Christian doctrine cover the end of all things and the dawn of everlasting life. He begins, sensibly, by discussing the meaning of the resurrection of the body.[7]

Beza asserts that when believers think of the blessedness of the resurrection, it strengthens them in their trials and tribulations and allows them to endure all manner of hardships because they keep in mind and sight their own future glorious resurrection. It, in other words, gives them hope. And hope is indispensable for a happy life.

Sin may have entered the world and death because of it through the First Adam, but just as certainly did life through the Second Adam, Jesus. Just as Christ rose from the dead, so will those who follow him in faith. Just as death for sin is real, just as real is life everlasting through the sacrifice of Christ. Death is a physical effect of the sin of the First Adam and resurrection a spiritual effect of the Second Adam's sacrifice.

Sin may well have been remitted in Christ, but Christians must still die. Nevertheless, this is no indication that redemption is not effective. Original sin, Beza observes, still inhabits believers and is not cancelled till death because that's when the struggle between the flesh and the spirit end. And second, shaking off this life makes living in the next life possible. Death, then, is the stripping away of sin and the flesh so that perfection and the spiritual body may replace them utterly.

Death, then, for the believer, is actually a merciful act of God himself. It should be viewed as a summons to

7. All which follows in this section is drawn from Beza, *Propositions and Principles*, 390ff.

eternity rather than as a punishment for sin. And, in fact, cannot be punishment for sin, since Christ has died for our sins himself.

The lost, on the other hand, do die in their sins and because of their sins and do suffer the everlasting consequences of their decision to reject redemption. They too rise again so that "their bodies may be reunited with their souls" so that they might not escape the full pain of the punishment their sins deserve. The whole body, then, rises again. Not just the spirit. And not just the flesh. The whole person that lies down in death stands up in the resurrection.

The dead who die in Christ go to the presence of God in heaven, and the dead in trespasses and sins go to hell.

> The same bodies that lie down shall rise, but not in the same qualities, as the very same body of Christ which was crucified and buried did rise, but not having those same qualities which it possessed at his burial. Yet this is the difference: the body of Christ experienced no decay, and therefore did overcome the power and effect of death, even in the very house of death. But our bodies are delivered from corruption which seemed to have been able utterly to have abolished them.[8]

The resurrection will take place in a flash, at the second coming of Christ. Beza says nothing about the intermediate state between one's death and resurrection other than to condemn the adherents of the notion of "soul sleep." He provides, regrettably, no theory of his own. At least not in the present volume.

The natural body is transformed into a spiritual body, as Paul affirms (in 1 Cor 15:35ff. NKJV):

8. Beza, *Propositions and Principles*, 393.

But someone will say, "How are the dead raised up? And with what body do they come?" Foolish one, what you sow is not made alive unless it dies. And what you sow, you do not sow that body that shall be, but mere grain—perhaps wheat or some other grain. But God gives it a body as He pleases, and to each seed its own body. All flesh is not the same flesh, but there is one kind of flesh of men, another flesh of animals, another of fish, and another of birds. There are also celestial bodies and terrestrial bodies; but the glory of the celestial is one, and the glory of the terrestrial is another. There is one glory of the sun, another glory of the moon, and another glory of the stars; for one star differs from another star in glory. So also is the resurrection of the dead. The body is sown in corruption, it is raised in incorruption. It is sown in dishonor, it is raised in glory. It is sown in weakness, it is raised in power. It is sown a natural body, it is raised a spiritual body. There is a natural body, and there is a spiritual body. And so it is written, "The first man Adam became a living being." The last Adam became a life-giving spirit. However, the spiritual is not first, but the natural, and afterward the spiritual. The first man was of the earth, made of dust; the second Man is the Lord from heaven. As was the man of dust, so also are those who are made of dust; and as is the heavenly Man, so also are those who are heavenly. And as we have borne the image of the man of dust, we shall also bear the image of the heavenly Man.

What sort of body will it be that is raised? We do not know, Beza insists. And goes on to say that he has no interest in knowing, no curiosity at all regarding the what and how of the resurrected body. The only thing he is willing to assert is that the resurrected body shines. Thus those bodies will be of a more "refined substance" than they presently are.

The bodies of those who will spend eternity in hell, on the other hand, will be suitable for the unspeakable torments they will experience forever. The implication is clear: those sentenced to hell will feel quite intensely every bit of misery their tormented bodies experience.

Everlasting Life

When Beza discusses everlasting life he begins by defining life. What is life? In Beza's estimation it is the power of the soul to enliven and move the body. One is alive when one is animate.

> To live eternal life is to be in that state wherein the elect, after the resurrection, are most joyfully joined with Christ their head, knowing God in heaven along with the angels, in a manner altogether unknown to us in the present, to enjoy his presence, and to glorify him eternally.[9]

Eternal means something which has a beginning but no end, Beza remarks, though properly speaking eternal means without beginning or ending. Everlasting is the term Beza means, though he fails to use it.

And concerning questions for which there is no scriptural answer, Beza thinks it best to omit them. What God has revealed in Scripture, he asserts, is sufficient for our salvation, and that is all we need to know. God has prepared things that neither eye has seen nor ear has heard of and we could and will never comprehend them until we experience them.

9. For this and what follows, cf. Beza, *Propositions and Principles*, 397ff.

God gives us all of the blessings of eternity because he has chosen us in Christ, before the foundation of the world, "from whom as from the head this blessed immortality does flow in a most full sort into his members that are joined to him."

Beza concludes his treatment of the doctrine of everlasting life in the presence of God as the special blessing of the elect as follows:

> The particular reason for which eternal life is given to us is this, that we may praise him eternally for his immeasurable and infinite mercy.

So, at the time appointed by God himself, we shall take possession of everlasting life. To attempt to calculate the day when this is to happen is "extreme madness." Our part is simply to await it knowing that it will be nothing short of perfect blessedness.

And just as everlasting happiness awaits the saved, the elect, so too does everlasting misery await the damned. Beza writes:

> This most horrible state is called the second death, not because the soul is separated from the body, or that the soul and the body of the damned experience death as the end of their existence; but because the body is putrefied and the soul is sentenced to eternal pain, being separated from God's favor and subjected to his everlasting curse.

It strikes moderns as a bit jarring that Beza's last word would be on hell. But he was a child of his day. And he cannot fairly be held to the standards of modern sensitivities. He, as so many other theologians of his day, was bound to remind the elect of the fears of hell. Hell was a fearsome deterrent to sin and sinners were regularly reminded of its pains and torments.

Theodore Beza asserted both the doctrine of heaven and hell, believed both were real, and informed his students of those facts. He wished the elect to enjoy the blessedness of their election and he wished the damned to know their everlasting fate in advance.

QUESTIONS FOR DISCUSSION

1. Do you think that Beza was right to see the church and state as partners in government?

2. If you had lived during Beza's day, would you have liked the church's influence on the state?

3. The understanding of Beza about heaven and hell seems very harsh. Do you agree with him?

4. Do you think hell is a real place and that people who are not elect will be there forever?

5. If you could talk to Beza about hell, what would you tell him?

10

THE ABIDING SIGNIFICANCE OF THEODORE BEZA

When we read Theodore Beza, we are transported back to a time, centuries before our own times. Beza was a highly educated, sixteenth-century theologian. His thought forms and ways of systematizing and expressing Christian truth vary in many ways from what we are used to reading by theologians today. Like all theologians, Beza reflected his historical context in the topics on which he wrote, his way of expressing (or "packaging") his theology, and what he considered most important for Christian persons of his own time to know and understand.

So we may ask: "What is the abiding significance of Theodore Beza" for Christian churches and Christian believers today? Are there important theological insights from Beza's teachings that can continue to strengthen and nurture churches and Christians today?

Beza was active throughout his life, both before and after he came to Geneva to assist John Calvin and the Geneva Company of Pastors (of which he was later Moderator) with ongoing reforms in Genevan churches. Beza established himself as a primary theological leader among Reformed churches. After his death, his theological writings continued to be significant resources and guides for the development of Reformed theology. So Beza was influential.

We believe Beza's insights can continue to be influential and nourishing for churches and Christian living today. His theological emphases can lead us to deeper insights into holy Scripture and clear understandings about the nature of Christian faith and the Christian life of service and devotion to the glory of God.

GOD IS GOD

We began this book by quoting a Bible verse from the Geneva Bible and a quote from Theodore Beza: "Whatsoeuer ye doe, doe all to the glory of God" (1 Cor 10:31 Geneva Bible, 1599) and "We are put in the world to serve the glory of God with both body and soul."[1] Serving "the glory of God" captured the purpose of life for Theodore Beza. Humans are created—and are given the gift of salvation by God's gracious election and predestination in order to serve God. God is our creator, the one who gives life and sustains life. The lives of humans are to reflect their creator and to be given to serve this God. Why? Simply because God is God.

Humans are to know God and to serve God. For Beza, theology helps us know who God is and what God has done. We are to study the Scriptures—in which God

1 Beza, *Sermons*, 480.

is revealed and made known—so that we may know the nature of God our creator. In Scripture we find who God is and learn of God's loving grace which elects us and gives us the gift of salvation through Jesus Christ. So we must know God in order to live the lives God wants us to live. God is God means there is no "higher being" and no other being who is to be worshiped, obeyed, and served—only the living God!

Beza's strong focus on God as God sets our understanding and direction in life today. First and foremost, we must know and worship and serve the living God in order to fulfill the purpose of our lives. God created us to love and serve our creator. We "let God be God" when we live in this knowledge of God—the knowledge of God which comes to us in God's Son, Jesus Christ, our Lord and Savior.

JESUS CHRIST IS KEY

Beza emphasized the person and work of Jesus Christ throughout his theology. Jesus Christ, as the Christian church has confessed was "truly God" and "truly human." Jesus was the incarnate Son of God: "God with us" (Matt 1:21) as God promised. In his life, Jesus obeyed God and in his death, he died so human sin could be forgiven. Jesus is the savior of those God has elected and called to be the people of God in this world. Without Jesus and all he did, humans would be forever—and hopelessly—lost and separated from the presence of God. Only through Jesus Christ can salvation, reconciliation, and peace with God be attained.

In Jesus Christ, we can see who God is and what God desires. In Jesus Christ, humans see how God wants us to live—in love and peace with each other. In Jesus Christ, we see God's purpose to save persons from the results of their sins and bring them into a relationship of love and trust with their loving creator. This was the passionate message Theodore Beza wanted to communicate to the world. Jesus Christ is key to the world and to all people. Only in and through Christ can humans live the lives God desires.

Through the work of Jesus Christ, God communicates God's will to humans. Through Christ's death, God communicates "that unspeakable love of God towards humanity because he sent his only begotten Son so that whoever believes in him might not perish but instead have everlasting life."[2] This is the central message of the gospel for Beza and it continues to be the key message to be heard and understood by all people today.

SALVATION IS GOD'S WORK

Like John Calvin and those in the Reformed theological tradition who came after him, Theodore Beza stressed that salvation is God's work. God eternally decrees salvation of those God chooses in election and predestination. While theologians presented different views of the "order of the divine decrees," the emphasis throughout—and what is of most importance—is that salvation is the work of God.[3] It is God who elects the people of God, and God through the Holy Spirit who calls and gives the gift of faith to the

2. Beza, *Propositions*, 167. As Wright put it: "Christ's death, according to Beza, was the focal point of God's benevolent actions for his people" (*Our Sovereign Refuge*, 207).

3. We have not entered into discussion of "the order of God's decrees" in what became known as "supralapsarianism" and "infralapsarianism." Beza is considered an early "supralapsarian." See Rouwendal, in Selderhuis, *Companion to Reformed Orthodoxy*, 589. Cf. McKim, *Westminster Dictionary*, s.v. "supralapsarianism" (309) and "infralapsarianism" (164).

elect for whom Jesus Christ has died. The Spirit illuminates minds and hearts and gives faith to sinners so they believe and love Jesus Christ as their Lord and Savior.

In the church's long history, various understandings of what is the work of God and what is the "human" work in salvation have been debated. But given Beza's views on sin and its debilitating power in which humans are "dead in trespasses and sins," humans have no powers (or desires) to save themselves from the death toward which their sins have led them. If humans are to be saved through Jesus Christ, it must be God who takes the initiative and gives the Holy Spirit to create faith in Christ in the lives of sinners. Salvation is the sovereign work of God and it is to God that all glory and praise for salvation is given!

For Beza, the Holy Spirit applies Jesus Christ to Christians, through faith. Faith, said Beza, is "an assurance that all Christians ought to have of their election and salvation, only by the grace and goodness of God in Jesus Christ. Faith and assurance is created, and daily increased by the virtue of the Holy Ghost, within the hearts of the elect, by the means of preaching the word of God, and the ministration of the sacraments. . . . So this faith is as the hand, which only receives and apprehends Jesus Christ to the salvation of those who believe."[4]

Salvation is God's work. Beza points us always to recognize the work of the Holy Spirit in bringing faith in Jesus Christ as the means of salvation. In Christ, we have assurance of salvation. All praise to God!

4. Beza, *Briefe and Pithie Summe*, 139.

QUESTIONS FOR DISCUSSION

1. In what ways do you seek to honor "God is God"—in what you believe and how you live?

2. What are ongoing ways in which Jesus Christ is key in your life—theologically and in daily life?

3. What comfort and assurance does recognizing salvation is God's work bring to your faith and life?

BIBLIOGRAPHY

PRIMARY SOURCES

Beza, Theodore. *A Book of Christian Questions and Answers.* London, 1578.

———. *A briefe and piththie summe of the Christian faith made in forme of a confession.* Translated out of the Frenche by R. F. London: Richard Serll, 1565.

———. *Briefe declaration of the chiefe points of Christian religion set forth in a table. Made by Theodore Beze.* Translated by William Whittingham. London, 1556.

———. *Confession de la foy chrestienne.* Geneva: Conrad Badius, 1559.

———. *De Praedestinatio doctrina et vero usu tractatio absolutissma.* Geneva, 1583.

———. *A Little Catechisme, That Is to Say, A Short Instruction Touching Christian Religion.* London, 1579.

———. *Master Bezaes Sermons upon the Three Chapters of the Canticle of Canticles.* Translated by John Harmar. Oxford, 1587.

———. *Master Bezas Household Prayers for the Consolation and Perfection of a Christian Life.* London, 1621.

———. *Sermons sur l'Historie de la Resurrection de nostre Seigneur Jesus Christ.* Geneva: Jean le Preux, 1593.

———. *Tractationes theologicae.* 3 vols. Geneva, 1570–1582.

Beza, Theodore, and Antoine de La Faye. *Propositions and Principles of Divinitie Propounded and Disputed in the Uniuersities of Geneva, by Certain Students of Divinitie There, Under M. Theod. Beza, and M. Anthonie Faius.* Edinburgh, 1595.

SECONDARY SOURCES

Backus, Irena Dorota. *The Reformed Roots of the English New Testament: The Influence of Theodore Beza on the English New Testament*. Pittsburgh Theological Monograph Series. Edited by Dikran Y. Hadidian. Pittsburgh, PA: Pickwick, 1980.

Baird, Henry Martyn. *Theodore Beza: The Counsellor of the French Reformation, 1519–1605*. Repr. New York: Burt Franklin, 1970.

Balserak, Jon, ed. *A Companion to the Reformation in Geneva*. Brill's Companions to the Christian Tradition. Boston: Brill, 2021.

Bray, John S. *Theodore Beza' Doctrine of Predestination*. Bibliotheca Humanistica and Reformatorica 12. Nieuwkoop: B. De Graaf, 1975.

Calvin, John. *Institutes of the Christian Religion*. Edited by John T. McNeill. Translated by Ford Lewis Battles. Library of Christian Classics. Philadelphia: Westminster, 1960.

Cochrane, Arthur C. *Reformed Confessions of the 16th Century with a New Introduction by Jack Rogers*. Louisville, KY: Westminster John Knox, 2003.

Geisendorf, Paul-F. *Théodore de Bèza*. Geneva: Alexandre Jullien, 1967.

Gootjes, Nicholas H. *The Beligic Confession: Its History and Sources*. Edited by Richard A. Muller. Texts & Studies in Reformation & Post-Reformation Thought. Grand Rapids: BakerAcademic, 2007.

Hillerbrand, Hans J., ed. *The Oxford Encyclopedia of the Reformation*. 4 vols. New York: Oxford University Press, 1966.

Letham, Robert. "Theodore Beza: A Reassessment." *Scottish Journal of Theology* 40 (1987) 25–40.

Lindberg, Carter, ed. *The Reformation Theologians: An Introduction to Theology in the Early Modern Period*. Hoboken, NJ: Wiley, 2001.

Maag, Karin. *Lifting Hearts to the Lord: Worship with John Calvin in Sixteenth-Century Geneva*. Grand Rapids: Eerdmans, 2016.

———. "Theodore Beza." *Expository Times* 126 (2015) 261–69.

Mallinson, Jeffrey. *Faith, Reason, and Revelation in Theodore Beza (1519–1561)*. New York: Oxford University Press, 2003.

Manetsch, Scott M. *Calvin's Company of Pastors: Pastoral Care and the Emerging Reformed Church, 1536–1609*. Edited by David C. Steinmetz. Oxford Studies in Historical Theology. New York: Oxford University Press, 2013.

———. *Theodore Beza and the Quest for Peace in France, 1572–1598*. Studies in Medieval and Reformation Thought 79. Leiden: Brill, 2000.

———. "Theodore Beza, Reformer in Exile." In *The Theology of Early French Protestantism: From the Affair of the Placards to the Edict of Nantes*, edited by Martin I. Klauber, 305–32. Grand Rapids: Reformation Heritage, 2023.

Maruyama, Tadataka. *The Ecclesiology of Theodore Beza: The Reform of the True Church*. Geneva: Librairie Droz, 1978.

McKee, Elsie Anne. *John Calvin on the Diaconate and Liturgical Almsgiving*. Geneva: Librairie Droz, 1984.

———. *The Pastoral Ministry and Worship in Calvin's Geneva*. Geneva: Librairie Droz, 2016.

McKim, Donald K., ed. *Dictionary of Major Biblical Interpreters*. Downers Grove, IL: InterVarsity, 2007.

———, ed. *Encyclopedia of the Reformed Faith*. Louisville, KY: Westminster John Knox 1992.

———. *The Westminster Dictionary of Theological Terms*. 2nd ed. Louisville, KY: Westminster John Knox, 2014.

Mohler, R. Albert, Jr. "First Person: Can a Christian Deny the Virgin Birth?" *Baptist Press*, December 24, 2003. https://www.baptist press.com/resource-library/news/first-person-can-a-christian -deny-the-virgin-birth/.

Muller, Richard A. *Christ and the Decree: Christology and Predestination in Reformed Theology from Calvin to Perkins*. Repr. Grand Rapids: Baker, 1986.

———. *Dictionary of Latin and Greek Theological Terms: Drawn Principally from Protestant Scholastic Theology*. Grand Rapids: Baker, 1985.

———. "Theodore Beza." In *The Reformation Theologians: An Introduction to Theology in the Early Modern Period*, edited by Carter Lindberg, 213–24. New York: Wiley, 2001.

Olson, Jeannine E. *Calvin and Social Welfare: Deacons and the Bourse française*. Selingsgrove, PA: Susquehanna University Press, 1989.

Raitt, Jill. "Beza, Guide for the Faithful Life." *Scottish Journal of Theology* 39 (1986) 83–107.

———. *The Eucharistic Theology of Theodore Beza: Development of the Reformed Doctrine*. American Academy of Religion Studies in Religion 4. Chambersburg, PA: American Academy of Religion, 1972.

———. "Theodore Beza." In *Shapers of Religious Traditions in Germany, Switzerland, and Poland, 1560–1600*, edited by Jill Raitt, 89–104. New Haven, CT: Yale University Press, 1981.

Rogers, Jack B., and Donald K. McKim. *The Authority and Interpretation of the Bible: An Historical Approach*. Repr. Eugene, OR: Wipf & Stock, 1999.

Selderhuis, Herman J. *A Companion to Reformed Orthodoxy*. Edited by Christopher M. Bellito. Brill's Companions to the Christian Tradition 40. Boston: Brill, 2013.

Summers, Kirk, and Scott M. Manetsch, ed. *Theodore Beza at 500: New Perspectives on an Old Reformer*. Edited by Herman J. Selderhuis. Refo 500 Academic Studies. Göttingen: Vandenhoeck & Ruprecht, 2021.

Trueman, Carl R., and R. S. Clark, eds. *Protestant Scholasticism: Essays in Reassessment*. Carlisle: Paternoster, 1999.

Wright, Shawn D. *Our Sovereign Refuge: The Pastoral Theology of Theodore Beza*. Studies in Christian History and Thought. Repr. Eugene, OR: Wipf & Stock, 2007.

———. *Theodore Beza: The Man and the Myth*. Ross-shire, UK: Christian Focus, 2015.

www.ingramcontent.com/pod-product-compliance
Lightning Source LLC
Chambersburg PA
CBHW070727030726
47601CB00002B/164